HENRY MILLER, SPIRIT & FLESH

Wayne F. Burke

ISBN: 978-93-90601-97-4

First Edition: 2022
Rs. 200/-

Cyberwit.net
HIG 45 Kaushambi Kunj, Kalindipuram
Allahabad - 211011 (U.P.) India
http://www.cyberwit.net
Tel: +(91) 9415091004
E-mail: info@cyberwit.net

Preface

This is a book about the great Henry Miller and his work. All his "major" and some minor works come under discussion here. The book is divided into two parts, one-third devoted to FLESH, and the remainder to SPIRIT. On occasion the two motifs happily mingle. This is not an academic study as I am not an academician. I am a lay-person with an abiding interest in Henry Miller and his work. An interest I have indulged off & on for over forty years.

This is not a work of hagiography but of criticism. I am an admirer of Miller and his work but am not blind to his defects as a human being or as a literary artist. Part of what endears Miller to me is his "human, all too human," characteristics (to quote Nietzsche, one of Miller's idols). Along with the endearing traits are far less endearing ones, especially in the characterization of "Henry Miller" persona of his TROPIC of CANCER and CAPRICORN and BLACK SPRING, books written in the late 1930's. A persona that underwent transformation during the course of Miller's literary career (as did his own psyche). This "transformation," in his art and life, is the primary subject of this book.

INTRODUCTION

In 1973, when I was seventeen years old and freshman at the University of Massachusetts, in Amherst, Mass., I bought Henry Miller's SEXUS at the campus bookstore and started an acquaintance with Miller's work that continues to this day (48 years later). I began reading the book, while I was at University, to the exclusion of other books I was required to read for my classes. Subsequently failing to read any of the novels assigned in my "The English Novel" class, I received a big fat 'F' from the professor, who actually was bald and egg-headed. Tant pis. I never did get back to Elizabeth Bowen or John Hawkes.

My stay at the big U. was 1.5 semesters long. I dropped-out before I flunked-out. What happens when you make your own curriculum. I don't blame Henry Miller (or Philip Roth or Kurt Vonnegut, two other writers whose books captured my attention and time). The academic life was not my trip. Nor Miller's, by the way, who could have gone to Cornell but lacked the money, and did one semester at City College of NY before dropping-out and going to work for his father in the vater's tailor shop.

That summer, of '73, I ordered a 3 volume set of Miller's work from a Book Club which I was a member of—a poor member ("Henry Miller"-like, I never paid for the books). There was BLACK SPRING, TROPIC OF CANCER, and TROPIC OF CAPRICORN, all available in America, since 1961, though written in the mid to late 1930's. I began reading and then rereading the work. To me, the sexual frankness of the work was not the reason, or chief reason, for my interest in Miller's work, but—and odd as this may sound, it was the exoticism of Miller's language interested and intrigued me most. Here was a writer who made English sound like a foreign language. An exotic, a writer of stunning imagery and breath-taking surreal riffs; a magician whose prose cast a sort of spell over me. As another Miller reader once remarked, about his or her reading of CANCER, “it was one of those books you ‘live’ rather than read” (pg. 192, Hoyle, Arthur, THE UNKNOWN HENRY MILLER). I felt that way; felt the work in my gut as well as brain (felt it in my dick too: more on that later). I felt naked before it: as if stripped by the force of the raw and often brutal assault Miller’s work delivers to the senses. A writer who wrote not only from the head and the heart but, as he said, from the “solar plexus” as well.

Reading Miller at seventeen was a liberating experience for me. And every reading since has likewise proven liberating. I suspect that the next reading, should there be one, will continue my liberation. It is remarkable to me, and a bit frightening, how quickly I can slip back into patterns of conventional thinking. Reading Miller revives my wonder at life and the world. Miller was an unconventional thinker, a revolutionary in his oftentimes startling approach to prosaic subjects. He often seems merely contrary but his contrariness has root in his own systematic thinking, his delightfully skewed way of looking at things. He can still shock as well, even from a distance of eighty years. The job of art, he said, was to shock, to wake us up: that his work can do. Karl Shapiro called Miller a “wisdom writer” (Introduction to TROPIC OF CANCER). I call Miller a “contemplative writer” in that book after book he circles around his subject, which is, primarily, himself, or a self, approaching from different angles. Not content to present the exterior of a scene only, he must analyze and make it part of a larger whole, turning each microcosmic event to the macrocosm. A thoughtful writer. A religious writer. One who contemplates his place in the universe—or his lack thereof. A thinker who came to distrust wisdom and knowledge, which he called poor substitutes for faith; came to view surrender and acceptance as more valuable than knowledge. Faith in what? In Life, Miller says. A surrender to what is, and acceptance to the way it is. (Much more on Miller’s spiritual beliefs to follow).

The sex, of course, was another inducement to read. SEXUS is hot stuff. Flaming. For any age. The most graphic, in terms of the hydraulics of the acts, in Miller's canon. One fuck after another. You would think Miller would become boring, the reader satiated with descriptive hydraulics, but Miller is unceasingly inventive when speaking of or about the procreative act, each act differing by degree, circumstance, happenstance...The humor deflating the seriousness, even solemnity, of the acts; acts interspersed with thoughts, reflections, on art and creativity, also on the dilemma of the individual, such as Miller, on living in a conformist and highly regimented society. Without these interjections we would have something closer to what Frank Harris wrote, in his book MY LIFE AND LOVES, the story of a serial seducer. Without segues into such subjects, we would have a "one-handed" read, a pornographic work, boring (to me) because unimaginative, usually repetitive, and full of cliched writing; one-dimensional as well, appealing solely to the hormones rather than brain. Work that, in relation to literature, is as craft to art. (Unlike in these works of pornography, Miller does occasionally resort to euphemism.)

After publication of SEXUS (1949 in France) Miller's confrere, Lawrence Durell, wrote Miller and took him to task, calling the work "morally vulgar...a childish explosion of obscenity" (DURELL-MILLER letters). Miller was stunned by Durell's criticism (B. Kraft, HENRY MILLER, The Last Years, pg. 92). To the criticism of Durrell, and others, Miller later replied, "if it was not good, it was true; if it was not artistic, it was sincere; if it was in bad taste, it was on the side of life." Miller's subsequent reputation as "dirty old man" and "pornographer" came into vogue after SEXUS. Somewhat strangely, Miller himself, in a deposition to the French court—after the book was banned in France, stated that he had come to regard SEXUS as pornographic, but, NOT obscene (pg. 474, Jay Martin, ALWAYS MERRY AND BRIGHT, The Life of Henry Miller). The distinction is a subtle one. Obscenity was viewed by Miller as healthy, as regenerative, and bringer of much merriment, as from the huge phallic symbols that were part of fertility rites of primitive cultures (and still are). A health and merriment lost somewhere along the way to present pornographic "age of neurosis" as Miller refers to modernity.

There is, of course, as Miller's readers know, much much more in his work than sex and sexuality. "Sex is the last thing...compared to love," Miller told Barbara Kraft (HENRY MILLER, The Last Years, pg. 11). I have come to understand, also, as Miller said, that it was the whole character, whole psyche, he was out to represent—the entire human experience, the flesh and the spirit, equally parts of a whole, existing in the world symbiotically, not separately, and thus pertinent to the condition of the "whole" human being. The being Miller, as "Henry Miller," the narrative voice of CANCER, CAPRICORN, etc., inhabited. Sex and spirit are indissoluble, in other words. One cannot exist, healthily, within an individual, without the other. An imbalance of either creates an unhealthy, or psychically damaged, person. The sex-crazed are looked upon with suspicion and soon isolated within society. The religious fanatic arousing antipathy is marginalized from main-stream society. Miller, an imbalanced writer, was isolated and marginalized within American society. From the "clouchard," or "outlaw writer," Miller became in later years a seeker and would-be sage. The anger and violent language of the early Miller work dispensed with as he came to seek a gentle surrender and a higher consciousness, a search begun in earnest shortly before his writing of THE COLOSSUS OF MAROUSSI (1949).

I think it probably impossible, given the autobiographical nature of Miller's work, to write a critique of the work—which is the intent of this study, without bringing in a good deal of biographical information. In his writings Miller has so closely mixed fact and fiction they have become one and the same. The nexus between his work and life has been made impenetrable by Miller himself. A process of "bibliomorphosis" Miller biographer Robert Ferguson writes (pg. 190, HENRY MILLER, A Life). Miller was a consummate fabricator, the truths and lies inseparable in the forging of a mythologized Everyman. Such a mythologized version of one's life dissolves character in that the "I" becomes generalized, and as such can seem both profound and buffoonish, both aspects of Miller's work (as we will see). I am speaking usually of "Henry Miller," the persona, not Henry V. Miller, the man—though, as I've noted, the two are often inextricable.

FLESH

1.

TROPIC OF CAPRICORN, written in 1938, is the 3rd volume of a trilogy including TROPIC OF CANCER, published in 1934, in France (English version), and BLACK SPRING, published in1936, in France (English version).

We are with "Henry Miller," a persona, man of many faces; man of contradictions, singing, a little off key perhaps, but singing anyway, like his idol Walt Whitman sang in a century past. Miller is personnel manager at the telegraph company (Western Union) which he calls, among other names, the "Cosmodemonic Telegraph Corporation." Henry has a string of boys, cronies, all on the que vive for a piece of tail; all working the female messengers for a "free" fuck, before the company takes them on, or dumps them...With and around Miller is MacGregor, the doorman and a lawyer, and one of Miller's oldest friends (both lads of the 14th Ward, Brooklyn); O'Mara, Chief Assistant; Hymie the "Bullfrog, Jew Bastard," who operates the switch board; O'Rourke, the dick-less company dick (prostrate trouble); Kronski, the medical "Doctor"; Steve Romero, a "bull-like" leg-breaker; all united in a desire to screw everything they can get their hands on. Screw the company too—at least that is Henry's idea.

The "pestilential cronies," as Henry calls them. Characters, Norman Mailer noted, "extravagantly alive...eccentrics, prodigious and twisted men, vulpine, intellectually-addled, prodigies of vanity so swollen on their unique misconceptions that they stagger under spiritual elephantiasis" (Norman Mailer, GENIUS & LUST).

They're shits but shits' who stick together. There are also shits less central to the cabal, including the messenger, and punk, Curly, who steals left and right and is an "easy" touch for the boss, Henry, who, though employed, is almost always broke and generally improvident. Curly, abused sexually by an Aunt, is out to abuse any "bitch" he crosses paths with. A predatory stance not unlike Henry's, though Henry abuses conscientiously: he is a "nice" abuser, "gentlemanly"; he sends them away with a few bucks or at least a pat on the ass...

MacGregor the disillusioned lawyer and "low-brow," has a car he and Henry ride around in searching for "cunts." If they pick one up, they give her a drink and more. If a moron or wet blanket (won't put-out) they drop her off on the roadside to make her own way home. Sometimes the cantankerous MacGregor shoves the woman out of the car as it is moving. Miller seems to take some kind of vicarious thrill from the coarse and brutal behavior of MacGregor and some other cronies, like Stanley, "The Polish Assassin." Miller implies, through his association and devotion to them, that he too is as brutal, or as capable of brutality as they, but betrays the notion time and again by his somewhat delicate and fastidious nature. Loyalty is part of the Miller character. The loyalty learned on the streets of his old Williamsburg, Brooklyn neighborhood when he ran with the "herd," and kept the unwritten "code of honor," of the streets, whereby each extends loyalty to every other, deservedly or not. Miller was fond of saying he was a Brooklyn boy of the 14th Ward. He eventually called himself a citizen of the world, and a citizen of Brooklyn's 14th Ward too, but not a citizen of the United States...MacGregor advises Henry to get rid of the wife, Maude. A "battleaxe," MacGregor calls her, with a "sour-ball puss." Also advises, that if necessary, in order for Henry to free himself from the matrimonial bondage, to "drown" his daughter. Kronski, the "medical" doctor, also advises Henry to get rid of his, Henry's, "hatchet-faced" wife. Likewise, Stanley, Miller's oldest friend, who offers to get rid of the wife for Henry—on the sly... All Henry has to do afterward, says Stanley, is move from New York then keep his mouth shut.

The wife, Maude, is a "cold bitch," according to Henry. Hardhearted toward his friends, and a little too proper for Henry's taste. Previously Henry's piano teacher before the two became more familiar. (Henry a child prodigy at the piano who considered a career in music). Maude doles out money to Henry every Monday morning: enough for his car fare and lunches. Henry resents what he views as her stinginess: she lacks his generosity (which some might call "extravagance"). His resentment of the wife is no doubt exacerbated by his resentment of his mother, another "cold bitch" in his life.

In any case, it is a fuck or be fucked world. And tenderness is out, as is pity. Only hard guys and girls survive the slaughterhouse of modern life in the Age of the Crapulous.

Henry goes to the funeral of one of his "friends," not to pay respect but to borrow a few bucks from one of the mourners. It is too bad that "Luke" died, thinks Henry, but... Luke was never much anyway, thinks Henry; in fact, Henry is glad Luke kicked-off because it canceled the $150 Henry owed him. Henry also has thoughts, on way to the funeral, about Luke's sister: wonders if he will be able to "put the boots" to her—if she will maybe be more amenable to a rendezvous (in her vulnerable, mournful, condition).

"Henry Miller" walks the "cold, glittering, and malign" streets of the city, among "the immense frozen solitude of the million-footed mob." A man of the city, former boy from Brooklyn. Like an anti-Whitman Henry is. Whitman, who celebrated Manhattan (a far different place than the one Miller walked through), remarking upon its prodigious throbbing vitality, unlike Miller—he who deconstructs his native city, noting its "cold waste fire of electrical display," the meaninglessness of its "calcimined" streets of "dead stone and unintelligible motion." Like Walt, who styled himself a cosmos of yea-saying American exceptionalism, Miller becomes a city himself, within the city, which he feels apart from, separated, exiled from even, though buried, more or less, in the heart of it. In the clutches of the robotic Moloch. Monstrous Moloch of money: Manhattan, the "dead and wormy center" where the great herd is driven by "loneliness; breast to breast, toward the wall of self, frustrate, isolate, sardine upon sardine" (BLACK SPRING, pg. 203).

Though a cosmopolite, "Henry Miller" lives in a primitive world of soothsayers and prophets. A magical realm where sage or saint or sinner might be met around the next corner. The work often assuming the character of fairy tale. "The world...is essentially a primitive world ruled by magic" (pg. 129, TROPIC OF CAPRICORN). Henry himself lives the life of a child, but one "strangled and stifled by the mutual consent of those who had surrendered." Meaning, the parents, adults in general. This "strangled child" image is one Miller applies to most all his childhood friends, some of them once heroes and demigods to Henry: friends who were, sadly, he reflects, snuffed-out by the living corpses of adulthood, those who had died before being buried. Child-slayers who had killed off their own dreams and had lost the ability to imagine; who had died in life, a living-death, the only kind of death there is, Miller would later say, and the worse...Henry bears witness to the spiritual murders of his boyhood chums and playmates; their tragic and cruel demise, some of them dying as their elders had; that is, before they physically croaked...How he escaped the common fate will be the tale he tells in his 3-volume THE ROSY CRUCIFIXION. "Survival," as Miller biographer Mary Deerborn noted (HAPPIEST MAN ALIVE) is the theme of Miller's major works. TROPIC OF CANCER patently a story of survival as ROBINSON CRUSOE.

Henry meets Mona, in a Times-Square Dance Emporium; she is a Taxi-Dancer, dancing with strangers for money. She will become the great enduring, and frustrating, love of his life. She calls him "Hen" or "Val" (Miller's middle name is Valentine). During the course of CAPRICORN, dedicated to "Her" (Mona), Hen tries to take her inventory, but finds it slippery going. Mona has murdered her past by reinventing herself in so many guises, she has no stable personality but changes day to day as circumstances require. She is what a psychiatrist might label a "borderline personality," also an actress, on stage and off. A narcissist as well—something Hen knows a little about ("two narcissists take the vow of love"—pg. 161, Mailer, GENIUS & LUST). Mona has lied so often she no longer can tell the truth, it seems.

Subterfuge is her style...And Hen's inventory always incomplete, even the subsequently written 1600 pages of THE ROSY CRUCIFIXION, supposedly a book about Mona (real name, June Mansfield), "a bird wrapped in soft fur...with white full face, wide mouth, chalk white teeth; taut swanlike columnar neck, blue black hair...eighteen years old...or thirty." She the "lubet," Miller writes (pg. 342. TROPIC OF CAPRICORN) "the abominate...the sublimate."

About 200 pages into CAPRICORN, Miller introduces the Land of Fuck. Where "spermatazoa reign supreme" (pg. 203). Boarding the Ovarian Trolley, complements of Hymie the Bullfrog and his wife's ovaries, our narrator, adopting the pseudonymous "Samson Lackawanna" goes on a strange journey that ends at the Amarilla Dance Hall, where Henry Miller meets Mona, the future betrothed. The 35 page Interlude is a less interesting journey than that leading up to it, but serves as a sort of demarcation line separating the narrator's past and future. Samson, thinking that, through Mona, he would "find" himself, discovers, some seven years later, that he has completely lost his sense of a self. Discovers also that relationship with another cannot lead him to self—a discovery of the "final process of identification with the world" (pg. 150) and subsequent realization "of the uselessness of ties." Later in the book, Henry becomes Gottlieb Leberecht Muller, and joins Mona in an embrace like Siamese twins, living "glued to the ceiling," entwined like snakes at marble heat through a "long interrupted solstice" (pg. 224). Mona as a dark goddess of sex, combination Aphrodite and Medusa, gliding through cosmic realms ("world of Chronos and his ovicular progeny" pg. 286) under a dark star, polar & tropical, Satanic and Godly, Moon & Sun, Saturn & Venus...Another attempt by Miller to take on an identity that fits, and to wear it. The search for identity like the search for God, unending, and continuing throughout Miller's work.

Some of the stuff Miller serves up in CAPRICORN is heavily influenced by a book titled ESOTERIC BUDDHISM, by A.P. Sinnet, published 1883. A book Miller was familiar with, first reading it at age twenty-two then again while living at the Villa Seurat in Paris seventeen years later (pg. 296 Ferguson R., HENRY MILLER, A Life), listing it as one of the 100 books that most influenced him (Appendix I, THE BOOKS IN MY LIFE, Henry Miller). The book an investigation into occult phenomenon, and the astral world, purportedly revealing esoteric information on Buddhism. There are seven root races of humankind, the author reports, all seven destroyed by either fire or water (Atlanteans the 4th root, finished-off by water). Human beings cycle in a spiral progression, always in spiritual ascent, through a multitude of loci after death, including on planets spiritual and physical (earth). Some go to a sort of holding cell, or waiting room, called "Devachan," where they have a "rosy sleep." "A subjective isolation of each human unit," Sinnet writes of Devachan. A sort of holding cell, or waiting room, a rough kind of Buddhist Purgatory—an indeterminate condition of good feelings follows, each unit happy in whatever the previous incarnation made happy, until the spiritual monad (that of us which survives physical existence) moves on to another rebirth elsewhere...Consider pg. 319 of CAPRICORN where Miller states that artists belong to the X root race, and are spiritual "microbes" that are carried over from one root race to the next, always appearing during times of catastrophe or upheaval. Artists, Miller postulates, are beings apart because not part of the "physical, racial scheme of things" (pg. 320). A thought that has the flavor of ESOTERIC BUDDHISM, substituting microbe for monad. Of the seven root races Sinnet mentions, monads do flit from body to body, planet to planet, he writes. What resides in Devachan—a state of being, Sinnet makes clear, and NOT a location, is the essence of the late self-conscious personality of the deceased (what Buddhists call "mindstream"). In his book SEXTET, Miller imagines meeting the late Japanese writer Mishima there, and having a chat (1946, H. Miller, "Reflections on the Death of Mishima"). Also mentions Devachan a few different times in CAPRICORN...Also, Miller's ideas about our divinity may have root in ESOTERIC BUDDHISM'S notion that in the development of the 7th "round" of evolution (we are now in the 5th), humankind will reside with angels in some sort of divine state...It is not my intention here to discuss this difficult to understand text any further, but only to point out that Miller's reading fed his written rhapsodies—his inter-luminary stretches of prose that sometimes read like extended OBE's. "See you in Devachan, Joey" (pg. 374, Ferguson) Miller wrote to his friend Alfred Perles, in one of the last letters Miller wrote.

Concluding pages of CAPRICORN are some of the most powerful of Miller's work. He dissects the family unit of himself, sister, mother, and father. Calls himself the "Leaning Tower of Pisa"; sister "The Whipping Post," Father the "Snoring Machine," and Mother the "Pterodactyl in Human Flesh." Relates that, because his sister is a half-wit, developmentally challenged (an "angel...given the body of an idiot"), he felt the need, the necessity, as a boy, to become a giant. His gigantism ensured that, because "she (sister) does not grow, I grow like a mushroom; because she has no personality, I become a colossus" (pg. 327). The potency of the pages is echoed in Miller's later written SUNDAY AFTER THE WAR (1941), containing an essay by Miller written after his return to the family after being away, in France and Greece, for ten years. Finding each member diminished: sister "shrunk and withered like a Chinese nut"; parents "two mummies...galvanized into a semblance of life" (pg. 327). A sense of "overwhelming compassion" for their diminution causes Miller to break into uncontrollable sobbing, he reports, and continue to sob, on and off, all during that night of his return.

CAPRICORN a worthy successor to CANCER. In CAPRICORN Miller seeks no less than revelation as to the true nature of reality. "A deeply satisfying amalgam of social criticism," writes Robert Ferguson, "personal confession and pure raving" (pg. 376, Ferguson).

BLACK SPRING, published in France between CANCER and CAPRICORN, and originally titled "Self-Portrait" (pg. 293, Jay Martin, ALWAYS MERRY AND BRIGHT), reaches the heights of its sister publications in half of its ten pieces. In this work it becomes clear that when Miller is writing about men, say, standing on a street corner, he means all street corners and all types of men standing—this is the "timelessness" he speaks of elsewhere, concerning his work. His city is meant to stand for all cities through time and all civilizations crammed in, from primitive to present. The sense of one river, Hudson or Seine, standing for all rivers, everywhere; he sought the universal in the particular, sought to merge his feelings, as a modern-era man, with all feeling-men, in an effort to be relevant, or understood, by the Mohammedan or the Christian or Chinaman, or whomever...Lawrence Durrell, speaking of Miller, said that "a real book," is a "tentative chance one takes on the infinite." Miller took that chance, again and again; it is what gives his work a sort of cosmic feel...By reaching toward the macrocosm from the microcosm he acknowledges the universe as well, and writing of a particular person, or himself, he attempts to relate person or self to all humankind. A style, or strategy, which is at the root of his artistry. Part of his Weltanschauung. From the particular to the general. Part of his genius, perhaps...He thinks of food, for instance, in particular, but also general sense: how it is served, how eaten, where eaten, who eats it; how the food is made, how distributed, the source of the food...Why is food scarce for some, and plentiful for others? And so on. A facility that has led to Miller being called the "cosmological man"—in his hand the tiniest ordinary thing or subject can grow into something universalized. Something that reaches for, if not touches, the universe.

In CAPRICORN Miller aligned himself with the Surrealists. Breton, Aragon, Tzara, Ernst, Vache, Jarry, Apollinaire, etc., finding their reaction to life similar to his own. In BLACK SPRING he becomes an official Surrealist through the section titled "Into the Night Life." An extended riff, a "Coney Island of the Mind," mixing dream, nightmare, fantasy, and elements of unconscious processes in a vacuous stew tasting of rational and irrational elements. Flavored with dream-logic. Miller recognized the Surreal as a legitimate reaction to the insanity of the First World War and to a general neuroses of modern life. In the face of such slaughter, as occurred in the war, reasonableness became suspect. Miller never did really join in the ultra-foolishness of the Dadaists (the sound poems of Kurt Schwitters, for example) but he was with the movement anarchically in spirit. Dreams are an elemental part of his work, and he recognized the power of imagery and symbolism of Jung's theories of the unconscious. The surreal and the poetically rhapsodic mix and mingle throughout Miller's early work.

2.

The first of Miller's novels was, reportedly, lost. CLIPPED WINGS was written in 1922 during a three week vacation Miller took from his job as Employment Manager at Western Union. Writing up to 8,000 words per day, Miller reports the book "a colossal tome...faulty from start to finish" (pg. 34, CAPRICORN). Reportedly about twelve messengers Miller came to know through his work (loosely based on Theodore Dreiser's TWELVE MEN). His attempt to write an inverse Horatio Alger book. Parallel with the twelve disciples is obvious, and suggestive, of Miller as Christ, a new Christ for a new age.

The second of Miller's efforts, his novel MOLOCH, written in 1928, contained sections from CLIPPED WINGS, according to Mary Deerborn (THE HAPPIEST MAN). MOLOCH was followed by novel #3, CRAZY COCK (also '28).

MOLOCH is a good book, but not a good Henry Miller book. So far beneath his greatest work that Miller, I assume, must have been embarrassed by the work, but could not bring himself to destroy the manuscript. Which was discovered in the UCLA Miller archive by Miller-biographer Mary Deerborn, and published by Grove Press in 1992.

Despite the book's flaws, the depth of its author's mind, broad cultural knowledge, and intellect, is impressive. Its main flaw is that it is not TROPIC OF CANCER. Other flaws include a slap-dash narrative style, episodic and self-consciously literary. Like CANCER, the plot is solely based on the peregrinations of MOLOCH's protagonist, one Dion Moloch.

Moloch is as ubiquitous in MOLOCH as "Henry Miller" in CANCER, though there is less of Moloch's internal life revealed: he remains somewhat hidden behind a mask of personality. The cronies and peripheral characters grab center stage (thus revealing themselves). Moloch seems incomplete, facsimile-like; Miller had yet to find the voice in which to reveal himself, the voice of "Henry Miller."

MOLOCH is written in the 3rd person omniscient. Dion has the characteristics and mannerisms of "H. Miller," persona of the TROPICS. Same foibles, obsessions, though with slight variation. Dion the bitterer, and less accepting; also, tries to be a legitimate tough guy, thinking of starting fights. A machismo "Henry Miller" fortunately lacks. Dion carries on in the Millerite fashion, as unfeeling, faithless, hard-guy; but, unlike Henry, Dion justifies himself to the readers. Less a reprobate in some ways though with far less backbone than his spawn.

There is the same Millerite love of obscure words in MOLOCH as in other Miller productions: "whilom," "rataplan," "noctambulo," "rutilant," "stribilious," etc...There exists, also, as in later work, some of the same cast of characters. Dion's wife, Blanche (Maude elsewhere) has her say in this early rehearsal for CANCER. She is not sex-object, as in SEXUS, but a disagreeable long-suffering spouse who nags her husband, relentlessly, objecting to his being absent from the house at night, and his attitude, of bitter derision, toward her. Dion comes and goes as he pleases, spending his nights after work (he too, as "Henry Miller," an employment manager at Western Union) with his boys, and girls. Many of the "pestilential cronies" of Miller's work show up in the narrative, and most have their say. Scary but literate Stanley, "Polish Assassin" of THE ROSY CRUCIFIXION (real name, Stanley Borowski) talks through an entire chapter, relating a tale to Dion and Prigozil (Dr. Kronski of later work). Dave—Hymie of CAPRICORN (real name Sam Satterson), hangs-out with Dion: a chapter describes their bacchanal to Greenspoint, to meet with two "malapert sluts"; Curly the Punk, of CAPRICORN, appears as Leslie...Even a Mona lookalike, one 'Naomi,' makes a cameo…

Patches of brilliance strain through some pedestrian prose: "...barbaric jazz deafened their ears (Dion and his black secretary out on a date in a Harlem nightclub) floods of rain-drenched melodies poured forth from the powerful epileptic figures on the dais. From the sluggish, drugged couples on the floor a peculiar aroma emanated, as from the marriage of camphor and patchouli. Notes like deep wounds, gushed over them in founts of dragon blood."

Blanche, the wife, becomes more than a shrew and less cardboard character toward the end of the book. Her assertion, earlier, that her husband is "hypersexed," is given credence when it is revealed that Dion has had sex with Blanche's mother; that during the honeymoon Dion screwed his mother-in-law while staying, with Blanche, at the in-law's home. That Blanche knew of the liaison, but never spoke of it, is a revelation to Dion that changes his attitude toward her and brings a reconciliation, lasting until further developments cause Blanche to flee the brownstone, with their daughter, and move elsewhere. The story of marital turmoil, told in the last three chapters, is a decidedly Dreiserian turn in the narrative, along with Sherwood Anderson-like touches of poetic imagery of plucked heartstrings (of both partners). The finale revives and rescues MOLOCH from ignominy, and shows that Miller, had he choose to continue in the elegiac mode, could have competed with both aforementioned writers in stories of heartland drama. (But Miller wanted to work otherwise—not in the "genealogical" style of Thomas Wolfe either, which he disliked, but in a more "vital" vein, which he did, in CANCER).

CRAZY COCK is a variant of the story told years later by Miller in NEXUS, Vol. 3 of THE ROSY CRUCIFIXION. "Vanya" in the earlier book, instead of "Stasia"; "Hildred" instead of "Mona"; and H.M. himself played by Tony Bring. An odd name. What does Tony bring?

Stanley, the Polish Assassin, shows up as Dredge; all the other familiar cronies of Miller's fantasia make cameos, but unlike other productions, merely pass through. It is all Vanya, Hildred, and Tony: ill-matched, misplaced, actors on a stage that slowly, over the course of 200 pages, shrinks to pin-point size.

It takes Miller until Part 5, over a hundred pages in, before he starts to cut-loose in the novel. Starts to sound, not Tony Bring-ish but Henry Miller-ish. Starts to cut the rug, in other words—a free flow of language a la BLACK SPRING and other works. The account becomes hilarious; drops the tragic line it was walking and turns progressively anarchically comedic and farcical. Real and surreal mingle, only not in a Dali tableau but a Buster Keaton film. A bowdlerized Sodom & Gomorrah, THE MOVIE, directed by Cecil B. DeMille and staring the 3 Stooges and Hedy Lamarr. Stark hilarity and crying jags. A loony Bohemia with bourgeois curtains in fake windows. Restraint goes out the fake window into the meadow next door where the amputated feet are buried. The only thing keeping the narrative from exploding, a la CANCER is the 3rd person omniscient Miller had tied himself to. That goddamn Tony Bring! Without him, the book would float like an air balloon filled with laughing gas!

Opium dreams and smoke too (never mentioned in NEXUS). A deeper and in many ways richer telling of Miller's menage a trois days in Brooklyn, provided later by NEXUS. In hindsight, CRAZY COCK makes NEXUS seem somewhat staid. Identical scenes in both works, but NEXUS lacking the gusto of many of the accounts in CRAZY COCK.

Tony Brring! peddles newspapers and sells his blood. Vanya makes art and is taken care of, as is Tony, by the efforts (gold-digging) of Hildred, who leaves Tony, her putative husband, for days at a time before returning, and then without explanation...Somehow, she keeps the ship afloat, by hook or crook. Tony remains in bed, often depressed, often immobile...Meanwhile, the prose soars in surreal flights above the quotidian. Part 6 is some of the best writing in Miller's oeuvre.

The great advance Miller made in the writing of CRAZY COCK was, as Mary Deerborn notes (Introduction to CRAZY COCK) his coming to knowledge of autobiographical romance as his genre and himself as subject.

3.

The persona, "Henry Miller," in SEXUS, and elsewhere, is like that of a god. A god with a prick. Whom women worship. They cannot get enough of him or his whang. And if not stroking his dick, the women are stroking his ego (and vanity, which is considerable). They "make a fuss" over him, take care of him as if he were a child. And Henry delights in their so doing. Likes it, even if he does not give a shit about any of them, excepting Mona, the "love" object. The women are "cunts" collectively and singly; at his disposal, and, if they make a scene, become disagreeable, a good reaming brings them around again; or, as last resort, a good clout, like Henry occasionally gives Maude, the wife.

The women are like "fuck-machines" needing only to be oiled, well-lubricated, to be put into working order. Whenever so adjusted, the women forget the little god's vices and deficiencies. So what if he is a scoundrel and scamp? So what if he does not pay alimony or the rent or even the restaurant bill? Allowances must be made for gods, even minor ones like our "Hen."

What is it that makes Henry so godlike? What is his secret? How did he arrive at omnipotence? In CAPRICORN he tells us that he learned, at an early age—around 12 years old, how not to care, which, is the secret of his demigod status. Not to give a damn...It happened after his little friend, Jack, another Brooklyn boy, became deathly ill and Henry, for a time, paid regular visits to Jack, until he, Henry, became "disgusted" and began hoping Jack died. Died and thereby ended not only his, Jack's, suffering, but the suffering his illness caused others, like Jack's mother (and like Henry). Thereafter, Henry wrote Jack off, and a few months later Jack died. While at the funeral, and sporting his new attitude, Henry tells us he cut a big fart while standing at the casket. An action appropriately symbolic of his new found ability not to care, which, he claims, allowed him a new "freedom," emotional freedom—allowed him to dance while others were busy dying (and he thus becoming, eventually, "the happy rock. "). A stance, he acknowledges, which may be cruel, even "inhuman," but Henry admits, in CANCER, that he is inhuman. Wants to be thought of as such. Says he belongs not to the human race but to the inhuman one—to those outside time, belonging to another epoch—a race apart.

When Mona, yet to be Mrs. H. Miller, attempts suicide, Hen, aware that Mona may or may not live, decides to remain with Maude (in his old home where he received news of Mona) and continue an orgy. Not caring, or caring too much, has freed him to act thus. To participate in an orgy while others are committing suicide...Again, when Peckover, the English proof-reader on the Herald Tribune, an acquaintance of Henry's, falls down an elevator shaft and dies (CANCER), Henry is unmoved. Peckover's actions, after he hit the bottom of the shaft, illustrate to Henry the farce that death can make of human life—how it can render absurd any notion of dignity attached to it. Peckover, with all his broken bones, reportedly got to his knees and began a fruitless search for his new set of false teeth. An action Henry and his crony Van Norden share a laugh over. His false teeth! (Besides, Henry is now in line for Peckover's job.)

Early in his account in SEXUS, "Henry Miller" is with "the widow," as he calls "Carlotta" (who, in "real" life, was "Delores," Miller's first live-in romance. A woman 14 years older than himself). Carlotta has an ill son Henry's age (TB). After the widow, Hen takes-up with Maude, and marries her (one child results, a girl). Maude the prude, and frozen ex-Catholic School girl. The marriage lasts seven years and ends after Hen meets "Mona," the taxi-dancer. "Actress" and fabricator (liar), the essence of vagueness, ambiguity, also a hustler of sorts, attaching herself to characters of the demimonde, as shady as herself. One of whom, "Pop," a cripple, she duns for enough dough to enable her and Stasia (introduced in vol. 3, real name Jean Kronski) to go on a trip to

Europe, leaving, for the time being, thirty-four year old Hen, (who moves in with his parents, and calls himself "the Ghost"). The money paid by Pop was "earned" by Mona who passed-off MOLOCH, the novel, as her own work, Pop paying her for the pages she "wrote."

Miller's frank use of commonly labeled obscene words and sexuality is old hat in this day and age (2020) of readily available raunchiness, 24-7. A time when main stream movies and social discourse are full of the language Miller brought from the streets into his books. An era of the main-streaming of vulgarity, and the "obscene" that formerly turned people away from the work (and to it as well). I do not think this the case any longer. I think that the reason some people turn from Miller's work—will not have his books in their home even, is the persona itself. People judging the persona, or personality, "Henry Miller," rather than the work itself. Unable to see the breakthrough of a new form, that CANCER introduces—a blend of innocence and experience in a rich patchwork that moves backward and forward or on a present time continuum. Unable to hear the extraordinary voice, street-wise and book-smart—a voice of power, unheard since Whitman. The book is judged on "character," the persona labeled "Henry Miller," an unapologetic and brash character; a moocher with a sense of entitlement; a user of others, friend and foe alike; a beggar but a haughty one, not stricken by conscience either...Dislikeable... An ASSHOLE. Who could put up with such an ego-driven monstrous personality? (Even with the charm and joie de vivre?) Only those who needed what he offered. Needed to see or be near the defiant example H. M. set in the face of a world and system out to destroy individuality. The "Henry Miller" who failed to get in lock-step and march. March like most everyone else. March wherever the world or the government said to march...Henry Miller rejected the work-a-day world, refused to take a job he could not interest himself in. (CAPRICORN an "extraordinary autobiographical indictment of...the American work ethic" Deerborn, pg. 19). Miller refused to join the military (marries 1st wife to avoid the draft—WW I), rejected notions of nationality, claimed himself anarchist and citizen of the world. A man without home or country. Refused to be a joiner with or without Georgie Babbit; refused to wave the flag (any flag). Called education "a form of leprosy" and said morals are "for cannibals" (pg. 156, THE TIME OF THE ASSASSINS). Scorned "ism's." (Nationalism a "farce" and patriotism a "fraud" pg. 156, ASSASSINS). Particularly Americanism. Insisted that America not a country but an idea. Called it a "woman's country," and warned that America would one day destroy the rest of the world. "America...produced gunmen and beer barons," not literature, he wrote. "Literature was left to women. Everything was left to women, except womanhood" (pg. 157, CRAZY COCK).

An uncompromising stand that extracted a heavy price from Miller: near starvation and almost total marginalization. Plus scrutiny by powers that be (FBI), social isolation, and, eventually, not fame but infamy.

SEXUS is a throw-back to pre-CANCER writing; Miller reverting back to the fabulous realism of CRAZY COCK. Abandoning, for the most part, the surrealism of earlier work: less a somnambulistic narrative; less dream and use of imagery from the unconscious; less depth as well...The book takes a distressing nose-dive about 100 pages from ending. Loses focus somewhat and lurches from scene to scene seemingly indiscriminately. Tired prose, flaccid, worn-out, juice-less...The wad shot, the tone senescent, attitude blasé...The sex scenes like tropical hangovers when compared to earlier fuck-fests...But the book makes a comeback through the saving grace of the great Burlesque House scene. The narrative saved from nullity. Though the "Osmanli" story does the thing in again...The book ends with shades of one of Miller's early idols, Knut Hamsun (others being Nietzsche and Frank Harris), as our narrator becomes a dog. Or, something less than a man…

"A great cake that fails to rise," Mailer wrote of THE ROSY CRUCIFIXION (Genius & Lust). Certainly, less artistry involved in production. Though there are sections— particularly in NEXUS— that rise to the height achieved in the TROPICS, Miller runs hot and cold through much of the three volumes.

4.

A number of writers have come to Miller's defense over the "pornographer" charge. Erica Jong, Norman Mailer, Anias Nin, to name the most prominent. Jong opines that the sex stuff is put in by Miller purposely in order to shock the reader. She may have got this notion from Miller himself, who wrote, in THE AIR CONDITIONED NIGHTMARE (1945), that the function of the artist "is to wake us up...stimulate our imaginations" (pg. 168). Miller biographer Arthur Hoyle (THE UNKNOWN HENRY MILLER) notes that the sex descriptions, told in "comically hyperbolic language" are a cut-up, a satire of the acts, and thus removed from the realm of "obscenity." Which, I think, true most of the time, but, on occasion, the satire loses its edge, as in a ten page description of a threesome entered into by Henry, Maude, and Elsie the girl "from upstairs" (SEXUS). The scene turns boring, cliched, repetitive, and tedious. Loses the humor inherent in much of the sex stuff, and the satire. "Assumes the tedium that characterizes pornography" (Mary Deerborn). Becomes, as Nabokov said of pornography, "cliched copulation..." I wonder what Miller was thinking about when he wrote such pieces (there are others); wonder if he was not writing with one hand only.

The threesome, or menage a trois, usually of Henry and two females, becomes a sort of motif of the works. Henry, Maude, and Elsie; Henry, Irma, and Dolores; Henry, Agnes, and Francie; Henry, Mona, and Stasia; and, in "real" life, Henry, June, and Anais.

Miller obsessed on the subject of sex. A little touched perhaps, on the subject. "I was a hopeless lecher," "Henry Miller" remarks in CANCER. Ida Verlaine, of SEXUS, says "you're a lecher" (pg. 179) when addressing Henry, who, after Ida's husband Bill, Henry's "friend," has left for work, urges Ida to stick a candle up her "twat" (which she does) then unbuttons his fly, and "gobble, gobble, like a hungry buzzard," (pg. 182) Ida has "it" in her mouth. The scene goes on almost as long as the scene featuring Henry, Maude, and Elsie, but is saved from cliché by an outrageous humor and satirical vein lacking in the longer scene.

Mary Deerborn remarks on Miller's questioning of his sexual identity throughout his early life (Introduction, CRAZY COCK), and Erica Jong (THE DEVIL IN PARADISE) claims Miller experimented with homosexuality with his "country friends" Joey and Tony (see CAPRICORN) from age 7 to 12. Deerborn seconds Jong, claiming that in old age Miller revealed "very casually" that he and Joey "had acquired the habit of buggering one another" (Deerborn, pg 34). She does not note the source for her remark. She also mentions Miller's time spent, in childhood, as member of the "Boy's Brigade," a sort of precursor to Boy Scouts. The group chaperoned by a certain "Major Tillotson," who had the habit of groping and fondling the boys in his charge...If this information of Deerborn's and Jong's is correct, it would have set in motion the obsession with matters sexual and given Miller his dose (no pun intended) of sexaholism, discoloring his attitude toward sex and toward himself.

Curiously, the grouping of the boys is mimic-ed in CANCER when Henry and Fillmore take a trip to Le Harve to meet their mutual friend, Collins, an ex-sailor and self-admitted pedophile. The three go to a gay bar where, Miller writes, they "enjoy the homosexual rout" (pg. 184, CANCER). Also, the threesomes of two males and one female, like that of Henry, Ulric, and Irene; Henry, Ulric, and Lola (Henry inadvertently grabs Ulric's "pecker"); Henry, Carl, and the "whore" in QUIET DAYS IN CLICHY; and Van Norden, Henry, and the "whore" in CANCER, recreate the triangle of Tony, Joey, and Henry, in the sense that, according to Deerborn, Tony refused to participate in the "buggering." Henry plays the "Tony" roll, as observer of the acts.

5.

PLEXUS is nearly without the sexual hijinks that figure so prominently in its predecessor. The first two-thirds of PLEXUS is vintage Miller, the work having an affinity with CAPRICORN in that both contain childhood and adolescent memories that Miller makes subject to his artistry.

PLEXUS records the nascent growth of Henry Miller, personally and artistically. Miller in the coils of nemesis and his chief-constrictor, Mona. The cronies come and go, among the "real" friends, O'Mara and Ulrick. Some perhaps solely out of the imagination of Henry Miller. MacGregor and O'Mara (Joe O'Reagan) seem interchangeable, as do Osiecki and Crazy Sheldon: the former couple standing for brutality, sentimentality, and craftiness, the latter for the insanity of obsession. Miller the only "real person in a world of ventriloquist's dummies" (pg. 332, Ferguson), who makes the dummies spokes of a wheel he is the center of. A center he tries to share with Mona but she will not stay put; is too flighty, lacks gravitas; has no fixed purpose except to dote on her "god," Henry Miller. She begs him to quit his job at the Cosmodemonic Telegraph Company, and he does, walking out one day without so much as a "goodbye." He is thirty-four years old and now has time and leisure to write in earnest, while Mona supports him. But he can't write. The stuff won't come and he lacks the discipline and order to produce; is too self-conscious, he admits, and confuses the "mastery of technique with creation" (pg. 58).

Unable to sell anything he does produce, he hits upon the idea of the "mezzontint," a prose poem of sorts printed on a colorful card, the cards sold door to door, or wherever...Henry has a hard time selling and so does bosom buddy O'Mara, so Mona steps in, has her name put onto the cards, as author, and makes the rounds of the village, selling.

Meanwhile, Henry continues trying to write, but is too paralyzed with fear to write well: afraid that, should he expose his "real" self, he will be "mutilated." He does most of his writing in his head, and the "books" take shape in the imaginations of his friends, all of whom believe in Hen's genius and in the books he will write, or could write, if only…

One-third the way through we come to a 22-page dream sequence that is, by turns, hilarious and frightening. The dream invests the narrative with another level, the subterranean unconscious of the surrealists and of Freud and Jung. The irrefutable dream-logic replaces, for a spell, the rationality of everyday life, the quotidian of landlords, jobs, newspapers, money, sublets, etc…

Following the dream, the book opens itself in tremendous vistas of thought and vision. A shift in consciousness, communicated in deeper measure than previously. Though the quotidian remains the same hustle to stay afloat in, the "I" of the narrator undergoes transformation, as, consequently, do his surroundings and associates. Everything invested with a kind of "magic," for lack of a better word. We swim now in an effluvium ethereal, where past and present are conjured in a sort of dreamscape. Where the little world the narrator inhabits, his microcosm, is suddenly put under a microscope and is seen the reflection of the huge outer-verse which, in turn, re-reflects the microscopic elements of the Lilliputian world...The story Miller tells shifts gears, as from a comic strip to an epic prose poem; from balloons of speech above the heads of characters to iambic pentameter, Al Capp to Chaucer.

These ethereal outbursts parsed between sections dry as unbuttered toast. Henry and his "real" friend, Ulrick (Kronski too?), enjoy each other's company, but the reader less so, as Ulrick is duller than the other birds of Henry's flock.

Mona and Henry attempt to run a Speakeasy. One of the customers, oddly named Caccicacci, tells a story of a robot invented in the 14th Century which had magical powers. The story encapsulates Miller's spiritual views: the uselessness of knowledge compared to faith ("Faith in everything..." pg. 415). The desirability of "acceptance," leading to the summum bonum of existence, Love. (We will visit Miller's spiritual notions in consideration of his COLOSSUS OF MAROUSSI.)

Otherwise, it is life per usual in Brooklyn for Hen, with or without Mona. Brooklyn, "city of the dead, the near dead, and the deader than the dead" (pg. 514, NEXUS). Attempts to escape the city, for life elsewhere, end in disaster. A trip to Florida to cash in on the real estate boom leads Henry to sleeping on a park bench, a sleep he is woken from by a whack of a cop's nightstick. In Virginia, chasing another scheme, of O'Mara's, Mona and Henry pause at Harper's Ferry while Henry sings praises of mad John Brown, the butcher of Pattawatomie Creek, hailing the old reprobate—dozens of court cases relating to his shady business dealings, and whose only success in life was his dying, as a great Liberator. (Swallowing the transcendentalists' line—Thoreau and Emerson, hook and sinker. To his credit, Miller does later wonder if Brown did not hurt the cause of black Americans, rather than help.) In Virginia they go bust, and return to the city, eking out an existence, living like refugees...Mona becomes a waitress, Henry an encyclopedia salesman. Mona facilitates a meeting for Henry with a soothsayer, a young Rimbaud-type, who informs Henry that he, Henry, is of the Mongol race, and part of an ancient brotherhood of seers—a race apart from the normal mongrel one. A special destiny is to be Henry's, but only after much suffering, says the soothsayer. Henry is thrown for a loop by the info. The tawdry world of NYC suddenly becomes a rambla of god-seekers mingling like crazy Russians out of a Dostoveskian day dream...Henry snaps out of it, comes-to in Coney Island (old "Sodom-by-the-Sea") after falling asleep on the subway, and minus his brief case and wallet...He returns to Mona, working as waitress at the Iron Cauldron. Enter, stage West, Anastasia Annapolis, a cherubic wanderer whom Mona adopts; she a "special" person, "unfathomable," Mona says; a "superior being." "Stasia" soon becomes a fixture in Mona's life and then in the apartment Mona and Henry share.

Henry continues the struggle to accommodate "self." His struggle to find, or become, as he writes, the "I of my I." For the nonce, he is stuck in the he, she, and we of it; stuck in the tradition of letters, and trying to accommodate plot, character development, atmosphere, and what not: form, in another word: the form to conform with the literature of the past, with literature, capital "L."

Meanwhile, waiting on the "threshold of eternity" (pg. 612), and finding, in Spengler, in the German's DECLINE OF THE WEST, proof positive of his, Henry's, intuitive notions that the Western world is doomed, and on the way out, unless a new outlook, a new being, is born (because the old is bankrupt and hopeless to change). A philosophy, or morphology, as Miller writes, right up Henry's alley. He takes the work in like a revelation. A new gospel. As he had his first exposure to Nietzsche. Likewise, to the work of Elie Faure.*

A human with a "cosmic consciousness" is called for; able to communicate mystically as well as through the "sterile intellect" (pg. 630), as the "dawn" man of the past could, Miller claims. A man or woman who has opened the eyes of their soul! Who has not rejected the world, nor renounced it...Sounding like the Miller of the COLOSSUS, Henry talks of finding peace, not the "peace that passeth understanding" but the peace of a man able to reconcile himself, IN THOUGHT, with the condition of the world...One who has intuited "true reality," which is the knowledge that "eternal life is not life beyond the grave, but the true spiritual life" (pg. 634).

From discussion of Spengler, which dominates the end of PLEXUS, we are plunked down in the midst of Dostoevsky at the start of NEXUS (Miller's big 4: Spengler, Dostoevsky, Hamsun, Elie Fauve). Dos as Mona's god, and Henry's kindred soul. To one "Stymer," a lawyer Henry visits (to sell a suit; he still runs errands for his father) Dostoevsky summed up the modern age—as Dante the Middle-Ages. In his work, Dos catalogued the death of "soul," which left post-modern humankind with Mind only. And being Mind only means the doom for humankind, Stymer continues, because humans are meant to be "whole," meaning both soul and mind. The same conundrum D. H. Lawrence bathed in: need for a new being, a new consciousness, since the old is played-out, bankrupt (we will come to Lawrence when considering Miller's THE WORLD OF LAWRENCE).

NEXUS features the menage of Mona, Stasia, and Henry. Henry leads a phantom existence as marginalized intellectual desperado. His wife's life taken over by her putative lesbian lover, Stasia. Henry lives daily with the loss. Like an angel exiled from Paradise. Though he tries to win redemption, all his strategies fail, and he becomes, more or less, a "buffoon." A fool. One who "believes despite everything" (pg. 38). A thirty-something year old "failure." A sleepwalker with head in a cosmic realm, eye on immortality and venturing like a sad Ulysses on the plain of daily revelation.

Hen's mother, the "shrew" (in real life, Louise Nietling nee Miller, a childish house-tyrant "given to rages that could last for days," Deerborn, pg. 22) lends Hen and Mona money to start a speakeasy, but the joint soon fails; meanwhile, his relationship with Mona, the "walking theater," begins to sour due to presence of Stasia. Hen begins to live life in a vacuum, minus company of his wife. "An endless void," he complains, drifting through the pages of the book, while Mona, meanwhile, comes on as Vampira: lip rouge, green eye lids, white powdered cheeks and wearing a cape...When she insists on carrying "Count Bruga" about with her—a "leering degenerate-looking puppet" (made by Stasia) that "grinned...like a skulking lout" (pg. 23, CRAZY COCK), Hen shits a brick, and brick by brick begins to build the edifice of the TROPICS, spending afternoons in the library with the "masters" and nights walking Broadway ("old Neon hell's afire"), and holes in the walls like Weehawken, Hackensack, Canarsie, White Plains, Timbukto...

Hen wonders if he has lost the ability to love. Considers "love." The mystery of it. As mysterious as energy, he concludes; which, like love, has always been...He speculates that love and energy may be one and the same; that the energy propelling the universe may be love itself...Ergo, love cannot be lost! It is inextinguishable. Or is it? To live solely in the mind is to have given up the idea of love, he opines. And mind is a vacuum—the "dread mind-machine" of thought! That sucks the unhappy reveler down into a bottomless pit, an "endless void" through which "one drifts and slithers in full waking consciousness" (pg. 42, NEXUS).

A suicide attempt by Henry turns farcical.

Their apartment, formerly a laundry, is like the inside of a bug house: Henry hanging about, Mona and Stasia carrying on...Kronski, the doc, comes by to examine Stasia (recently sprung from the loony bin) and tries to rape her during examination...A dementia praecox atmosphere of suspicion and paranoia evolves. "Like sequences to a coke dream," Henry remarks (pg. 67).

Wandering around the city, searching for a job to do, Henry's experiences with secretaries and sub-species of bosses read like Kafkaesque mimicry, part nightmare, part burlesque...He tires crashing his way in, as he did in becoming employment manager at Cosmodemoic...But it's no go for our lad, until, with Saturn turning off to another aspect, Henry runs into Tony from the old neighborhood, the former "little dago," who made good as a political boss. Hen is given a job with the Parks Department, and is soon writing speeches for his boss.

Henry's problem is how get rid of Stasia? And recapture or reignite Mona's love?

A problem, constantly on Henry's mind, that becomes academic when the pair bug-out, to Paris, leaving Hen to himself...He moves in with the parents, sends money to Mona in Europe...She returns, and alone. Hen and Mona set up shop, again, as a couple. Mona brings home the bacon but Henry can't cook (write). Missing the old "I" of his "I." But "Pop" is on the horizon and Mona reeling him in. He with the shekels to pay for Hen and Mona to escape NY to Europe. Money due as soon as Hen can put finishing touches to MOLOCH (see chap. 2).

By the end of NEXUS our narrator is on the verge of becoming pure spirit, inhabiting like a phantom the phenomenal world. In the fictional Millerite chronology, NEXUS leads directly to the opening pages of CANCER, wherein "Henry Miller" evolves from would-be writer to literary artist.

(* note. Elie Faure, 1873-1937, Frenchman and doctor, polymath, writer on diverse subjects, best known as an art critic and for his monumental HISTORY OF ART, published in 4 volumes, between 1909 and 1927.

Miller's numerous references to Faure and his, Miller's, lumping Faure in with such luminaries as Dostoevsky, Blake, Nietzsche, and Spengler, baffled me. Who is Elie Faure, I wondered. By going to his work, I found out. Found out why, after I'd read HISTORY OF ART, Miller included Faure in the pantheon above. The work a tremendous prose poem, epogee, paean, celebrating the accomplishment of art & artists, and thus, of humankind as well, as the two, in Faure's cosmology, walk hand-in-hand. A humanistic quasi-scientific investigation, neo-Lamarckian—meaning following the ideas of Lamarck, founder of an evolutionary biology favoring a cooperative life within species rather than Darwin's ideas of survival of the fittest. (Faure does not deny the cruelty and occasional monstrous aspect of nature; in fact, equates the cruelty and monstrous as part of artistic creation—part of the aesthetic process of the creator (human and godly).)

Art is Faure's thesis, life his subject. An integrator, synthesizer, of evolutionary ideas in conjunction with the history of artistic production by societies and individuals, ancient, modern, and between. Faure links humankind and nature through charting, in outline, via sweepingly broad judgments and vision, the development of artistic styles & forms and evolutionary forces, proposing along the way that species and cultural transformation evolve together, and through a cosmic unity of some kind. A connection between organic and inorganic forms, which, to Faure, implies a united cosmos.

The scientific Lamarckian discussions of less interest to me than those on art & artists. Faure states that art is immoral, or unmoral, "not once does it (art) offer even a veiled protest against the power of woman, the injustice of man, or the indifference of the gods." He calls artists "monsters" of creation (as I have stated), a notion Miller revives in TROPIC OF CANCER, referring to himself as "inhuman," as belonging to a race apart—those outside time, belonging to another epoch (than modernity). Belonging, incidentally, without morality, or a morality different, at odds with the rank & file. (To Faure, morality divides, while art, he writes, unites.)

Faure believed the greatest art resulted from the strongest dynamic of energy (spiritual) and love. A belief Miller echoes in NEXUS. "Art the expression," Faure writes, "of spiritual energy, created through the meeting of virility and love." Spiritual power, passional power, and lyricism what the poet thrives on; what the race too, lives on. By accepting the elements of energy and love, civilization might ascend to its highest peak, which, Faure states, is "art."

I close this note with what might be the grandest, of many grand, statements Faure made concerning art & artists: : "Terrible as life may be, the existence of creative activity without any other end than itself is enough to justify it. The game evidently appears, at first sight, the least useful when we discover that it increases our enthusiasm for life and makes us forget death.")

SPIRIT

1.

Miller elected to leave Paris and France due to onset of WW II (1939). From France he relocated to the island of Corfu to stay with his English admirer and disciple, poet and novelist Lawrence Durell, and Durell's wife, Nancy. When the Durell's moved from Corfu Miller moved to Athens on the mainland where he met a number of literary figures, two of whom—Seferiades and Katsimbalis, feature prominently in the travel book Miller wrote of his Greek experiences, THE COLOSSUS OF MAROUSSI (1941). After his passport was invalidated by Greek authorities, Miller had little choice but to return to the United States, which he did, landing in New York, 1-1940.

Miller completed his "Greek" book after his return.

From Paris to Marsailles to Corfu to Athens to the Peloponnesus to Crete to Knossos to Phaestos, back to Athens, to Thebes to Delphi, back to the Peloponnesus, to Corinth to Sparta, and back to Athens. This the itinerary Miller followed on his vacation in Greece where, he says, he found "peace." At Epidauros particularly. Peace not in the usual sense of lack of conflict, but the peace that "passeth all understanding." A peace of the heart. A peace not "static but dynamic" (pg. 76). Peace which leads to joy. A peace available to all who give up attachment, which is the root, Miller opines, of the human "disease." Shit-can habits, ideologies, ideals, principles, possessions, phobias, gods, cults, and religion, he advises. Let it all go, because "whatever we cling to, even faith and hope" (pg. 78) keeps the disease latent. And look not to God for help either, Miller says. God long ago abandoned humankind. Did so in order that "we might realize the joy of attaining godhead through our own efforts" (pg. 78). God and the divine are within humankind's grasp, Miller insists, but it takes a mighty effort on the part of the individual to reach them. By becoming more and more conscious,

Miller writes in his later book THE AIR CONDITIONED NIGHTMARE, we "become more and more like God," and as we become more like God we can start to talk with God. "God will be with (us) all the time" (pg. 168). An individual striving, to become more conscious, and only an individual striving, because the intercession of religion does not, Miller writes, get us there. There in the clouds with divinity, and opening our wings, like angels, which, Miller insists, we are.

Through this new-found peace Miller claims a new freedom. Freedom in the knowledge that all conquest is vain, "even the conquest of self, which is the last act of egotism" (pg.205). The conquest of self as well as the reaching for God and the divine require a personal revolution by the individual against a way of life not his own—life predicated before his or her arrival. A revolt continuous and relentless is called for, is necessary to overthrow old ideas, ideas handed down and sanctified by tradition and society as a prescribed way of life, which we accept not knowing we have a choice in the matter, and thus become a part of something we had nothing to do with creating. We have not even joined of our own volition!

To throw off the fetters of one's existence requires an act of surrender. Surrender instead of conquest, Miller says. Giving up all our possessions, rights, classes, nations, peoples...Only then, through complete surrender, will things change, and the homicidal streak in humankind be erased. With revolution, of the heart, and surrender, the diseased world order will be changed. Hearts will "beat in unison," Miller writes, "with the great heart of the world."

Miller is not your average Joe tourist. He has no use for guide books, or guides, and scorns learned tomes of history—books that "stink of learning" (pg. 95). Henry depends upon his impressions and intuition. He reads the landscape like a human seismograph. At Mycenae he intuits "Cyclopean monsters washed up from the sunken ridges of Atlantis"; at Argos he sees, with his 3rd eye, Colorado and American

Indians—wigwams on the steaming plain; at Knossus he divines great eras of peace and joy; at Phaestos he is certain the place is, or was, the female stronghold of the Minos family—an abode of queens; somewhere between Delphi and Athens he decides that a certain pass is a place of great slaughter and murder...These are his impressions, and, right or wrong, he sticks to them.

Miller's growing interest in astrology, stimulated in Paris by astrologers of his acquaintance, extends in the COLOSSUS, with a long riff on the planet Saturn ("lymphatic globe of doubt and ennui" pg. 104), a few words on Virgo (Goethe, Miller writes, one of the best Virgo types ever) and a quip on Mercury "himself." Miller declares that one of his 'guides', and friend, Greek poet Seferiades, has strong Virgo traits. And deep into the book, Miller takes a side trip into the Armenian slums of Athens to visit a soothsayer versed in "Arabian astrology." The astrologer declares Miller a Capricorn of the Jupiterarian type; also declares that Miller will never die. (Jupiter, the planet that saved Miller from death after he fell through the skylight of his Paris apartment one night. The only planet in Miller's horoscope not badly "aspected" at the time of his fall. Miller relates the story of his fall in pages 260-5 of THE AIR CONDITIONED NIGHTMARE.)

About half-way through his Greek book Miller goes off track with a Boogie-Woogie exposition that is an attempt, apparently, at humor, but falls flat. The humor, however, returns in Miller's descriptions of his relationships with various Greeks. Like the vice-consul of Herakleion. A man who has written a book about Crete. A book he insists Miller read. Which Miller does—3 pages of it, before he tosses it aside, disgusted; but pretends, so as not to upset the man, to have enjoyed the work. A work the man continually speaks of, ad nauseam...During a visit to the consul, whose wife serves Miller boiled rice to cure his diarrhea, a visitor arrives—a Greek newly returned from America and full of praise for the country. Praise that Miller takes exception to and he begins a long and fantastic story—not only to rebuke the man, but to keep from having to talk about the Consul's book—a story that segues into an hilarious take-off on Wall Street and morphs into a parody of American manners, a delirium of dream and reality, an outlandish laugh-out-loud Marx Brothers meet Chaplin sketch…

In Greece Miller confronted the elemental: earth, air, fire, water: and the light, which, he writes, made everything Greek seem holy and natural. An illuminated existence: "synchronization of dream and reality." Miller felt himself nearer to the stars in Greece, more so than anywhere he had ever been; also, the ether more charged, he states, and an elixir or essence in the perfumed atmosphere. The place awakening a nostalgia for ancestral man and the days when gods walked the earth instead of puny specimens of "modern" man. Over-looking the plain of Messara, the world seems, to Miller, "ethereal, dream-like...a evanescent panorama"; coming upon the plain of Thebes, while in an automobile, he burst into tears; meeting the Herakleion prefect, he declares the man a "born leader," most powerful man he has ever met. Compares the man favorably, as leader, to Hitler and Mussolini and decides the Prefect could assume dictatorship of the Balkans, or the "whole Mediterranean world," with no problem...Clearly, Miller is high, intoxicated by the sights and sounds. Infatuated as well. His description of Athens under lights at night is a delirium of reporting. "Swimming in an electric effluvia which comes directly from the heavens." A rainbow, seen by Miller outside Argos, is the most "heartening, frivolous, gamboling rainbow" he has ever seen. His description of his other Greek poet guide and friend, Katsimbalis—who is the "COLOSSUS," make of the man a larger than life figure. Toward the end of the book Miller asks for forgiveness for his exaggeration, but immediately afterward qualifies all accolade by pronouncing the Greek poet the "most human individual" (pg.238) he, Henry, has ever met. A man "truly and thoroughly human." A reverent, generous, vulnerable, and voluble fellow, indeed.

To Henry, Greece is the center of the universe—giving him the feeling of being at home. The Greeks, unlike those of his native land, those Americans, are open, frank, natural, spontaneous, and warmhearted. The country itself the fountain-head of "wisdom and inspiration." And his experience of Greece has brought him, he states, face to face with himself and also cleansed him of hatred, jealousy, and envy. For which, he states, he is immeasurably grateful.

Because Greece is the home of the gods, who were "created out of the human spirit," a link between "human and divine" still exists in Greece, claims Miller, unlike in the Western world where the link is broken. A break that, in Miller's opinion, means inevitable destruction of "civilization" due to "skepticism and paralysis" (pg. 235). Man-sized Greece shows the way, to the West, which needs, Miller posits, to become smaller, slower, more human somehow, if it, the West, is to escape doom. The Greeks, Miller says, gave body to everything, thus "incarnating spirit...internalizing it," while Christianity, by emphasizing the soul in man, disembodied him. The "incarnated spirit," Miller writes, is shattered in the Western world through failure to internalize spirit in body (due to the malefic influence of Christianity). The West, in Miller's opinion, functions neither in the body or the spirit (hence, is doomed).

Miller did little to no writing during his months' long stay in Greece. He felt a kind of growing liberation develop and the idea occurred to him that creating more was inessential, and that serving the world, somehow, in "the highest possible way" (pg. 206) was essential. He got it into his noggin, or heart, if you will, the urge of passing from art to life, becoming more unselfish, more responsible, and moving toward the final expression: "mastery of life" (pg. 206). Becoming more like Jesus, in other words, or, the Buddha, or, Kirshnamurti, or, Lao-tse, men who turned their lives, and very flesh, into works of art, living art: became art in their being...Art, Miller continues, is only, like religion, a preparation into the way of life. To continue writing "beyond the point of self-realization" he writes (pg. 206), "seems futile and arresting." At the very end of his travelogue he states that he has decided to dedicate the rest of his life to the "recovery of the divinity of man," who is, he reminds us, an "angel." (The main problem being that we, humankind, forget we are angels, or don't even know it, and act like brutes.)

It seems that Miller, with the writing of the TROPICS and BLACK SPRING, reached the apotheosis of his creativity, and from then on, with minor exceptions, wrote by rote and habit. THE ROSY CRUCIFIXION strays far afield, parts pedestrian, parts brilliant. Nothing that Miller wrote after CAPRICORN forms anything like a satisfying work of art. Meaning the disparate elements combining to make a "whole." His novella, "The Devil At Large," comes close. So does COLOSSUS. But, clearly, Miller's art suffered proportionately to his spiritual "awakening" (or whatever happened to him in Greece). His stated desire to live more in the world, to identify himself with the world more, and, perhaps, influence it "at the core," clashed, it seems to me, with his creative endeavors (born-out by recognition of his inability, later, to rise to the level of quality of his early work).

I mean, after his annunciation, which, was not necessarily caused by his Greek sojourn, but did begin there, I believe, he became more a part of the world, a hero even, a savant to some (dirty old man and reprobate to others), a famous person in America after his banned books were published in-country by Grove Press in 1961 (or infamous), but, by becoming more a part of life, did he influence and help more people? For me, reading Miller was a liberating experience. Helping me to liberate myself from restraint and convention. Giving me license, urging me, to seek my own way to individuation; to seek more life not more things; to live more intensely not more cautiously; to dare to fail; to learn through living, not primarily by thinking about life; to distrust authorities and pedants in favor of my own intuition; to accept life and surrender to it instead of reject and fight against it; to try and become wiser rather than smarter; to give freely and just as freely receive; to try and change my heart not only my mind; and to seek not more work but more life...Life abundant. Without the earlier written books, however (TROPICS & BLACK SPRING and, heck, the COLOSSUS) would I have been impelled, through reading but the later works, to liberation? I doubt it. Without the first books Miller would be unknown today, or little known. To someone, like myself, who does not really "buy" Miller as a philosopher of much depth nor a trust-worthy guru or lama to the so-called spirit world (though a spirit of tremendous depth), the question raised above is definitely answered "no." While those who do find Miller a philosopher of depth and sage to the spirit world, and favor BIG SUR AND THE ORANGES OF HIERONYMUS BOSCH (1957) over the earlier work, will, no doubt, answer "yes." The question, in any case, is probably answerable by one person only: Henry Miller, who, contrary to the Armenian soothsayer's prognosis, died. Or did he? Certainly, his works, carrying his life-force, live on, and probably always will, so long as literacy and the written word exists. His words will live on so long as there are people refusing to buckle under to injustice and demand the right to walk their own path; so long as the revolution of the heart has not been won or the disease of humankind—our homicidal instinct, eradicated.

2.

Now that we have completed our tour of Greece, let's take a jaunt across Miller's bete noire, the good old U S of A, aka "America," shall we?

Henry Miller driving, Abe Rattner, artist (he and Henry met in Paris), riding shotgun. The car, a used '32 Buick bought with some of the 500$ advance given Henry by Doubleday & Co. in exchange for a book. A travelogue.

It is 1941 and America, or her President and Congress rather, is about to declare war on Germany. There is no Interstate Highway system, but plenty of service stations, real stations that actually fix your car, or try to (not the combo gas and grocery and nearly useless stores of today). Good thing too, because the car is temperamental, liable to overheating. During the trip Henry has multiple occasions to make acquaintance with mechanics. Men Henry likens to doctors, because both give prognoses, and different mechanics, like different docs, often contradict one another. A frustrating experience if trying to figure out the problem, car or body.

Rattner makes sketches: he is along for the ride only, because Doubleday has nixed the idea of including his drawings, along with Miller's prose, as too expensive a proposition for a book. (Too bad! Look at what a delightful element Franklin Booth's drawings added to Dreiser's A HOOSIER HOLIDAY.)

Whoa! Miller swerves all over the Holland Tunnel. Not only myopic and tending to absent-mindedness, Henry has just recently learned to drive. 49 years old and recent recipient of his first driver's license. Once out of the tunnel and an hour outside NYC, Rattner takes the wheel. He and Henry will share driving duties for the next 2500 miles.

The myth of America as opposed to its reality, as glimpsed out the car window, drives Miller to distraction. Supposedly, Americans are free of prejudice and hate; liberty-loving souls in a free democracy, noble people full of idealistic sentiment...Outwardly, a fine, upstanding people, in a bold masculine world...In reality however, inwardly, a "vulgar pushing mob," Miller writes, "filled with worms" (pg.42, CAPRICORN). "The country a whorehouse run by women...the native sons acting as pimps and the bloody foreigners selling their flesh..." A country both "pacifistic and cannibalistic" (pg. 42 CAPRICORN).

The dream and its shadow.

America is a place where the "poet is anathema, the thinker a fool, the artist an escapist, the man of vision a criminal," (pg. 24, THE AIR CONDITIONED NIGHTMARE). America "is prematurely old, as a fruit which rotted before it had a chance to ripen" (pg. 117). In particular, he has little use for the North of the country, equating the area between Pittsburgh, PA and Youngstown, Ohio, to Dante's Inferno. The capital of the "new planet," he writes, the one "which will kill itself off," is Detroit, Michigan (pg. 41). He prefers the South and Southwest to the rest of the land. The former for the graciousness of its people, the latter for its natural beauty ("nature gone ga ga and dada" pg. 239). Not that he is all that big on the South...Writing that only two of its cities pass mustard with him: Charleston, S.C. (though "corpse," its lower limbs "have been resuscitated" pg. 285), and New Orleans, though only the French Quarter. Miller finds Southerners more intellectually "scintillating" than their Northern or Western brethren. And though he finds many Southern cities hideous, ugly, and lifeless, he praises the gentility endemic to the South and the slower, more relaxed, and gracious manner of Southern living. Praises too the South's aristocracy, in antebellum days and in the diminished but proud condition of mid-20th century aristocratic hold-overs like Weeks Hall, caretaker of "The Shadows," an old mansion in New Iberia, Louisiana, where Miller spends some time. Weeks is exemplar, to Miller, of the defeated but unbowed Southerner; he is also, in Miller's eyes, an eccentric, and "character."

Miller likes characters. He is one himself, it goes without saying. The root of Miller's affinity is that "characters" are outside the American norm, non-joiners with the homogenized crowd and the annoying go-getters, some of whom do try and help, but usually make a mess of everything... Characters have a tendency to go their own way; as does Henry Miller.

Of the southern Negroes, whom Miller often refers to as "darkies" (my grandfather used the term), he makes only one remark. A curious one. "The Negro," he writes, "is the true owner of the land." He does not report relating this information to any blacks he meets. One wonders what the response would have been had he done so. (In COLOSSUS Miller wrote, "the great Negro race...keeps America from falling apart" pg. 137.)

In New Orleans Miller discovers a saint and sage in the personage of a 70-year-old surgeon who, at age 60, took-up oil painting. Miller is highly complementary of the man's painting, noting the influence of Cezanne. (A Horace Pippin-like piece is reproduced in the book.) To Miller, the man is an outsider par excellence. Miller praises not only the painting but the man too—the "whole" person. Being himself the quintessential outsider, Miller recognizes and celebrates others. For the "insiders," whose success and popularity have allowed entrance into a status quo, Miller has a great deal of scorn. Miller calls the work of Grant Wood "sterile stylizations." Thomas Benton he labels a "Neanderthal." (Only American artist Miller seems to have use for is "the wizard," as Miller calls him, John Marin. "Where is our Picasso?" Miller asks in some kind of snit-fit (pg. 128). Where is the American Van Gogh, Cezanne, Matisse, Braque, or even Utrillo? There may not be one, but there is Ryder, Pollock, De Kooning, Rockwell Kent, Andrew Wyeth, Louise Nevelson, Georgia O'Keeffe...Some of whom contemporaneous with Miller.)

Writing about Arkansas, Miller makes some preposterous remarks. Says that the comic and social critic Will Rogers, born in Arkansas, rivals in stature Abraham Lincoln. Really? Quips that the fact Arkansas fought on the side of the Confederacy is "another point in its favor" (pg. 134), a remark hinting at Miller's attitude and feelings about the War Between the States. Feelings he makes clear in the last chapter of the book (which I will discuss shortly).

Miller adds two razor-backs to his collection of exemplars. "Coin" Harvey, author of "The Book," a 19th century best seller (subject is usury), who set out, in Messianic mode, to save civilization by building a pyramid 130 feet high, somewhere in Arkansas. The structure, he hoped, would call the attention of the world to the fact, as Harvey saw things, of civilization's inevitable doom due to the selfishness of humankind. The pyramid supposed to somehow motivate or impel the world to action (what action, is unclear) and thus, save civilization. Coin took subscriptions out on his project but it was a case of "no-coin" or "not enough coin" and the thing was never built. Miller expresses love for the man because of the man's attempt rather than his execution. Miller loves all men called rebels and failures, loves them, he writes in his later written book THE TIME OF THE ASSASSINS, because of their "humanity."

The 2nd bird is a "reincarnation of Plato," grand and multi-linguistic Albert Pike, initiate in the mysteries and flub-dub of Freemasonry. Another would-be savior Miller elevates to his personal pantheon, for reasons obscure (to me). Miller quotes from a Freemason text remarks that sound like highfalutin' gibberish, but I cannot judge, not knowing quite what the Freemasons are all about, uninitiated into their arcane knowledge, not knowing the secret handshake, and not understanding their lingo...It seems, to me, that Miller's enthusiasm for the man is due to Pike's self-proclaimed and lonely standing as "citizen of the world," a status Miller also claimed.

With car engine steaming, Miller, now alone, Rattner having abandoned the enterprise, somehow reaches California via the deserts of Arizona. He then moves on to Hollywood, the "celluloid city" (pg. 244).

Invited to a fancy dinner party, attended by millionaires and celebrities, Miller gives account of the drunken feast, noting the politically reactionary talk of an "elderly thug in a tuxedo" (pg. 248), who had an "apoplectic fit" every time President Roosevelt's name was mentioned. His account a comedic tour de force, parodic, and as scathingly humorous as his speech, in COLOSSUS, to a confused Greek, on the nature of American go-getterism.

The aforementioned last chapter of Miller's book calls for a response. Beginning the chapter with a review of his time spent in the South, Miller continues on with a lament, for the Southern defeat in the war, and resultant devastation of the land, noting much of the devastation done by Sherman, who, Miller writes, cut "the path of a Vandal" (pg. 284). Lamentable also, to Miller, the fate of the South beset upon by the North, post-war. Which was, Miller writes, "a substitution of one injustice for another" (pg. 284).

Oh, really?

The "slave culture," Miller continues, of antebellum South ("culture" an innocuous word, no?) was but in its "first blossom," Miller writes. What could not have come out of such a "promising land" (pg. 286) he wonders. Mentioning Greece, Rome, and Egypt (all slave societies) he asks, rhetorically, if anyone would deny the value of the legacy these societies have bequeathed to us? A disingenuous question: one implying that antebellum South's system of chattel slavery was no different than the slave societies of antiquity. "Disingenuous," because untrue. Chattel slavery in the South was, UNLIKE the empires of antiquity, unique in that it was based on race. The only slave system in the history of the world, I believe, to be based solely on racial characteristics (until advent of the Nazi's 3rd Reich). Also, why should anyone lament the South, and the southerners who refused to give-up or even ameliorate their "Peculiar Institution?" A refusal that brought them devastation, and General Sherman—no "Vandal" but the war's avenger and liberator. And if lamenting is to be done, should not the lament be for the freedmen who, in the war's aftermath, were so quickly re-enslaved socially and economically by the duplicity of certain southerners and terrorism of the white supremacists organizations such as the Klan?

3.

THE AIR CONDITIONED NIGHTMARE was rejected by the mainstream publisher who had given Miller an advance. Nobody was willing to publish an anti-American screed while the country was at war (1941). The book was not published until 1945 (by NEW DIRECTIONS).

Marginalized in America—though not in France, where he was a literary celebrity—Miller managed to keep his head above water during the war-years and later. Mostly through loans from Anais Nin and others, plus through his "begging letters," asking for hand-outs, as well as through the small royalties paid him by New Directions which had published a handful of Miller titles, work deemed "safe" from the censorious, unlike his TROPICS and BLACK SPRING.

In 1943 Miller landed in California where he lived rent-free in a garage apartment made available to him by one of his admirers. In La-La Land he rubbed shoulders with a variety of swami-mistagogues, Fakirs (and fakers), new age gurus, enema-enthusiasts, and astrologers. Astrology and astrologers had begun to play an important part in Miller's life during his latter Paris years. Facing every decision, Miller first consulted his astrological chart for guidance, or had a chart drawn up (an action which, often as not, reinforced his state of indecision).

While in the garage apartment, Miller began to turn out watercolors which a local art store dealer put on display. To Miller's surprise, the paintings started to sell, bringing him a small income outside of the few dollars he made through his writing. At 50$ a whack, Miller sold 1400$ worth, over a year (pg. 233, Deerborn). (The price of his pieces later rose to 200$ a pop. Much later, 2000$. Much much later, 20,000$).

Through a series of serendipitous encounters, Miller left the garage for a shack on a ridge in Big Sur, along the California coast. Rent 5$ a month. The shack rented to him by an admiring reader of his work. From this initial shack he branched out to more commodious digs (though still without heat or electricity at this time).

His Big Sur, CA, experience lasted 17 years.

During his time there he completed NEXUS but produced only one other work considered "major," BIG SUR AND THE ORANGES OF HIERONYMUS BOSCH (1957), a work Erica Jong compared to THE COLOSSUS OF MAROUSSI as another "strong response to the spirit of a place" (pg. 308, THE DEVIL AT LARGE).

Before I handle the ORANGES I am going to spend some time doing an exegesis of a book Miller wrote in 1945 but was not published until 1956. At the time of writing this book, titled THE TIME OF THE ASSASSINS, a study of the life of the brat of French poetry, Arthur Rimbaud, Miller was living with a Polish/American woman named Janina Martha Lepska, a graduate of Bryn Mawr, who gave up her study of philosophy at Yale to marry Miller and move into the "shack" at Big Sur. She was 21, Miller 53. The couple's first child was soon on the way.

Miller's study of l'enfant terrible of French poetry, was published during cold war years, and the "Red Scare" in America. A time of paranoia and the threat of atomic or nuclear annihilation. A distinctly eschatological atmosphere. "Everyone waiting for the 3rd World War," Miller remarks (pg.35). The book written in '46, on the heels of Miller's spiritual awakening, or conversion, or whatever the nature of his experience in Greece. He was, at the time, newly armed with "God" and a desire to be more a part of the world and life; be less selfish as well, even if his art suffered for it.

Might be a good time to ask: Was his spiritual transformation "real?" Does not his conversion seem...a little too big a jump from the angry and egotistical persona "Henry Miller" of the TROPICS and BLACK SPRING to the loving Henry of the COLOSSUS, full of a kindly acceptance of life and its creatures? A man who was, seemingly, out to screw everyone, friend or foe, suddenly starts speaking of surrender and belief? In his study of Miller, GENIUS & LUST, Norman Mailer introduces, as only Norman Mailer can, a worm into the apple of Henry's "goodness," insinuating that the book was perhaps a ploy on Miller's part, written to appease the literary establishment, which had pronounced him and his work persona non grata. Win the applause and possibly the good grace of the old literary dinosaurs with a book that an old lady, a grandmother, Eleanor Roosevelt, or a nun, could read without being offended or blushing. A duplicitous act; a dishonest act: Could our Henry be guilty of such? A possibility, that much must be conceded. But, leaving aside literary/politico considerations, Miller hammers home his spiritual beliefs each time he steps up to the plate in his Rimbaud study, still trying, as in the COLOSSUS, to "invent a spiritual blueprint" as Mary Deerborn wrote (HAPPIEST MAN ALIVE, pg. 239), "by which connections between art and life can be understood." In this study we hear Miller's prophetic voice, full of gnomic utterances and his spiritual "truths."

"Our mission on earth (is) to combat false teaching by manifesting the truth which is in us" (pg. 145, ASSASSINS).

The voice of the would-be seer: "society has broken up into aggregations...The presence and worship of God—is missing" (pg 133).

The same voices heard in Miller's study of D. H. Lawrence as well (posthumously published. A book Mary Deerborn calls "unreadable"—she is right...More on this book, later).

The work also as much supposition as biography. Often more theory than criticism. And as much a study of Miller as Rimbaud, Miller walking side-by-side with the French adolescent genius, making of him a sort of alter ego, or trying to anyway. Comparing his life to the poet's, finding multiple similarities, affinities, correspondences, and writing, meanwhile, a spiritual biography as well. Charting his, Miller's, spiritual growth and matching it to Rimbaud's procession through his short life (37 yrs.).

Occasionally, Miller sounds like a priest. God is on Miller's mind and close to his heart. Who is God? God is "creation itself" (pg. 132) Miller writes. And available to all who seek him, Miller informs. Meditation not necessary, either. Those who struggle against Belief, stand with their backs to the light, "fighting their own shadows" (pg. 138). Only when the light comes over the nonbeliever does he or she realize that he/she must surrender pride & egotism.

Amen.

Not ordinary pride, when speaking of Rimbaud (or Miller) but Luciferian pride— both had in spades. Miller recognizing it as character defect in his spiritual about-face, but Rimbaud, never; which lead him to self-martyrdom, to throwing himself, Miller remarks, "to the dogs."

Renouncing poetry at the tender age of 19 or thereabouts, after writing A SEASON IN HELL, his caustic masterpiece (a book that runs the gamut of the emotional scale in writing rich with imagery of terrible beauty: "Damned by the rainbow...I fixed frenzies in their flight...eternity it is the sea mixed with the sun...may it come the time of love the time to be enamored of...") and after shelving his next book, THE ILLUMINATIONS, Rimbaud chucked the literary scene and jumped head-first into life, the world of commerce, of exploration, of practical men & women...and became, Miller writes, the "poet of silence." Existing, critic Wallace Fowlie remarked, "(not) as words on the page, but in the white spaces."

A renunciation, but, Miller insists, a kind of surrender and submission too: surrender to silence and darkness.

"Submission...permits one to dedicate his life, through devotion, to something beyond himself" (pg. 131), Miller writes. But Rimbaud did not devote himself to something beyond, but to the making of money, amassing a fortune, which, he believed, would win him "freedom." Which was an illusion, Miller remarks, because, he states, freedom cannot be obtained by external means.

Rimbaud became a wanderer, a drifter; "a considerable passerby," as Mallarme said. A big screw-up, Miller implies. If only he, Rimbaud, had acquired a "Master," Miller laments. (Like Jesus? But could even Jesus had helped someone whose dictum was "ni Matre, ni Dieu?")

At one point in his wandering, Rimbaud joined the Dutch army, and then promptly deserted. Made it to London a few times, also Brussels, Germany, and Austria, where he was escorted out of the country, and returned home to Charleville, "the inescapable umbilicus" (pg. 212, ARTHUR RIMBAUD, Jean-Luc Steinmetz), and to his mother. Again and again, to his mother and the boredom of the provinces, until rested and ready to re-start.

Back to mother even though he cannot stand her company for long. Why doesn't he dump the mother? Leave her? He can't, Miller says, because she is part of his history, and he is not ready to give that up. History, plus his desire—man's desire, to re-enter the womb, to find safety, security, in the amniotic fluid where "illumination and acceptance," Miller writes, "exist for the unborn." The bondage, felt by both Rimbaud and Miller, is the secret that "gnaws" at their vitals, Miller writes, giving them no rest. They spend their lives in trying to break the "fetters" (pg. 50) of their bondage. Not until they do come to terms with the mother—through acceptance, for Miller (a place Rimbaud never got to, Miller says) can they rid themselves of the fetters. Meanwhile, they are driven, and restless, rootless, trying to fit in somewhere but never succeeding. Failing to adapt or to integrate, they eventually become rebels, but their rebellion does not bring them the love they unconsciously seek, denied them by the mothers, and they remain dissatisfied.

The "black star" Miller calls Madame Rimbaud, "which attracts him (Rimbaud) fatally" (pg. 120).

Madame: stupid, bigoted, prideful, stubborn!

Sounds like a description of Henry's mother.

Madame drove her son "out into the world" Miller writes (pg. 139), by denying him and even persecuting him. A maiming of Arthur's "affective nature" (pg. 140) resulting in the poet becoming incapable of loving or receiving love. Instead of love, Rimbaud knew only pity, Miller claims.

Miller refers to the maiming as "a wound of separation." That runs deep, and bleeds Rimbaud, who, because he suffers a crisis of being, a lack of individuality, Miller posits (ambiguously), Rimbaud enters a "void of negation" and flounders...But still, he has his defiance. But the defiance, Miller writes, only saps his strength. And he drifts, rudderless, across the continent, to Germany, Austria, Italy, England, bouncing but always returning, to Charleville, place of his birth, and to mother, and rest and recuperation, then, armed with more than half a dozen languages he's picked up in the course of his travels, and his prodigious strength returning, leaves again (or returning to Roche, a village of one-hundred Rocheux, where M. Rimbaud inherited a farm from her grandfather and sometimes lived—Arthur called the place a "sad hole"). Makes his way to Aden, Djibouti, and Harra (Addis Abada) in Ethiopia where he sets himself up as merchant selling guns, gum, guano, whatever...And amassing his fortune. For ten years, and then, sick and dying, 40,000 worth of gold francs in his money belt (weighing 40 lbs.) is returned to France and enters a hospital in Marsailles, where his leg is cut off (cancer). Then to Roche, then back to Marsailles where, intent on returning to Harar, he is compelled to reenter the hospital, where he dies (his sister in attendance).

Miller had a renunciation of art for life, as well. But he did not, like Rimbaud, give up art completely—just adjusted focus. Turned the dial a bit. Rimbaud's renunciation was complete. Outside of an article he wrote for a geographic society publication, he wrote nothing else but letters. Letters in which he bemoans his fate, his lack of wife and family, home;

would not it have been some kind of compensation if he could have wrote, "I have my art"?

Miller's talk of God, soul, acceptance, surrender, and belief, does not mean he had adopted a religion. Not formally anyway. Religions are a "hoax" he writes (pg. 150). He makes a number of condemnatory remarks about Christianity in ASSASSINS and elsewhere. "The whole Christian interlude has been a denial of life, a denial of God, a denial of the spirit" (pg. 90). When Miller mentions God it is not the Christian or Pagan God he speaks of, he insists. It is, simply: "God." As for Christ, Miller considers him a great figure of history. An example of one of Miller's "whole" beings, a man who had no need of art because he was a work of art, art in the flesh. Also, someone who denied his individuality and hence, his egotism. A far cry, Miller says, from the present age, which has "reached the ultimate point of egotism, the atomic state of being" (pg. 37). Though Miller prefers Buddha over Christ, he refers to Jesus as "Lord and Savior." "Jesus was a mystic, a visionary, and his medium was the living word" (pg. 226, THE WORLD OF LAWRENCE, Henry Miller). Miller is a religious man but without a religion, which is the definition of a mystic or would-be mystic. Miller cherry-picked from world religions whatever he found useful as he attempted to "draw up a mystical aesthetic" (Deerborn, pg. 239). Also, as Robert Ferguson has pointed out (HENRY MILLER, A Life, pg. 100), Miller's "success as a writer would become ever more associated with the idea of a religious quest, in which art itself was the religion, and himself the Clown-Jesus at its center."

One of the ideas of Miller's aesthetic is that those who have risen, through their own effort, to God, have been rewarded with the divine gift of creation. Those on a high frequency of being, commingling with the divine, like the "masters," Blake, Nietzsche, Dostoevsky, were in the "glow" Miller writes, "of divine essence."

Singing God's praises, Miller states, "is the highest performance man can enact" (pg. 138). "God wrote the score...and conducts the orchestra." In COLOSSUS Miller claims that God has thought out everything in advance, and so "we have nothing to solve, it has all been solved for us." A bit of predestining that Miller echoes in ASSASSINS when he claims that the artist is only an instrument, and that man "creates nothing of and by himself." Writing elsewhere, of the days he wrote TROPIC OF CAPRICORN, Miller claims to have done little more than having taken dictation in the writing of that text. That the words were transmitted to him by a "Voice." He reports that he would say to the Voice: "Je t'ecoute...Vas-y!" (pg. 128, BIG SUR AND THE ORANGES OF HIERONYMUS BOSCH). The divine gift must have been his. It all sounds a little kooky. When Miller was writing the Land of Fuck section of that book, he says he became chagrined, aghast even, and asked the Voice if it were trying to get him, Henry Miller, into trouble. In SEXUS, Miller offers a slightly different "take" on this phenomenon, remarking that what sometimes happens is that his everyday "self," the one identified in public registers after death, is taken over by a "real" self, almost a stranger to the workaday self, who seizes the reigns, and is the one "writing in the air" (pg. 29, SEXUS). A "real" self that goes unrecognized by one's friends and intimates (who often write the condition off as a case of someone being "high" or out of his/her mind). In NEXUS Henry calls on the "archons" (pg. 131) after taking pen to paper. Those "mysterious entities...cosmic enzymes...at work in every seed...who engineer the creation" of everything. (Archon: 1. A chief magistrate of ancient Athens)...More on this phenomenon when we get to discussion of BIG SUR AND THE ORANGES.

Is Miller's fascination with the poetry and life of Rimbaud a case of "hysterical identification?" Do the "endless" parallels, as Miller calls them, add up to a similar character and spirit? Are Rimbaud and Miller truly "spiritual brothers," as Miller implies?

To start with, consider the mothers, whom we have pretty much already covered. Both of them domineering, "Northern" types, one referred to by her son as a "shrew with a caustic tongue," the other, likewise cold, stingy with her affection, ultra-respectable, a small woman of means (M. Rimbaud). The fathers are notable for their absences. Rimbaud's pere, a Captain in the French Army, deserted the family when Arthur was a boy; Miller's vater, though present, was insubstantial, brow-beaten by his wife who wore the pants in the family, and made himself scarce, preferring the bar room and his cronies to home-life. The ancestors of both writer's come in for a serious drubbing: Miller referring to his family tree as being made of "idiots" (his maternal grandmother, and an Aunt—his mother's sister, both institutionalized). And writing, in CAPRICORN, of "the stupidity of the blood tie" and emptiness of love "not spiritually imbued" (pg. 151). Rimbaud writing that he inherited his "small brain, awkwardness...and love of sacrilege" from his forebears, the Gaul's (though he never "buttered" his hair, he says). Both developed a hatred for the place of their birth, Miller endlessly castigating NYC, where he was lonely in the herd; Rimbaud showing little more than scorn for Charleville and Roche, city and village in a province in the extreme North of France, bordering Belgium, and to Rimbaud an intolerable back-water responsible for stifling him in boredom. Both sought early escape from the abodes of their sorrows: Miller out West, via train, age 18, landing in New Mexico and quickly disillusioned because the "West" did not look anything like he imagined if would. (After reaching California, he turned around and headed back East.) At 16, Rimbaud boarded a train that took him through Belgium and back into France (the Franco-Prussian war was in full-swing) where he ran out of money, was arrested as a vagabond, and jailed for a short spell (the mother said that if he "ran away" again, he be turned over to the "authorities." Pg. 49, ARTHUR RIMBAUD). As youths, both were scholastic over-achievers. Both were considered somewhat sissified, Miller's mother curling his hair and dressing him in a Little Lord Fauntleroy outfit. Taunted by other children, both developed hard shells in defense. Both began to rebel against the status quo, seized, Miller writes, "by the demon of revolt" (pg. 16), and quickly earning "bad boy" status; each indulging traits, later more pronounced, of insolence and arrogance; both, as young men, moved about restlessly, and usually on foot, Rimbaud all over the map, and Miller all over NYC and environs, once taking a trip to Florida, another to Virginia (by thumb). Seeking to make a living, both failed, finding their skills unwanted, unneeded (though Miller did hold, for 3 years, a job as employment manager at Western Union). Miller worked as clerk for a cement factory concern (Atlas Portland Cement Co.), assistant editor at the Charles Williams Mail Order House (fired after one month), for the Parks & Recreation Dept., NYC, as encyclopedia salesman, dish washer, garbage collector, and lemon-picker as agricultural laborer. Rimbaud attached himself to a circus, and also joined the Dutch Army; was a foreman of a work crew in a quarry; also became a merchant, selling everything (but not slaves, according to Steinmatz, ARTHUR RIMBAUD). Both, in adolescence, had a "heart-breaking" affair, Miller with his dream goddess, the untouchable and unapproachable "Cora Seward," and Rimbaud with a mystery girl, of, as he wrote, "violet eyes." And, finally, both have their time in Hell, walking with Satan, and admiring the King of the Rebels, Lucifer. But finding it hot, too, and not all it is cracked-up to be—that it can be downright uncomfortable for the overweeningly prideful. Like Miller in the Brooklyn apartment he shared with his putative wife and her lesbian lover. A time in "Hell" he wrote about in NEXUS and CRAZY COCK. Rimbaud knew both Hell and Paradise in childhood and adolescence, as he ran the emotional gamut like a prodigy and came out the other side with his book UNE SAISON EN ENFER, which records his deep ventures into hellish realms. Later, as a young man, he suffered the hellishly hot conditions of life along the Somali coast, roasting "as if in a lime-kiln," he wrote home in a letter.

The similarities, analogies, myriad, it must be admitted—though how much of the childhood and adolescence stuff applies to childhood and adolescent in general, in everyone's development? Don't most adolescents suffer angst and revolt by nature? I know I did.

What differs in the two biographies, is the outcomes of the lives discussed. After their seminal works were written—their "nigger" books (a word used by both writers), TROPIC OF CANCER and A SEASON IN HELL, which, for both, Miller claims, were works of "despair, revolt, and malediction" (pg. 47), they go different ways. Miller onto his spiritual transformation and renunciation of his earlier, more selfish, self, and Rimbaud into silence after his renunciation of art, and of his old self too. But the biggest difference, according to Miller, is that in his career Rimbaud turned from literature to life, and in his, Miller's career, as writer, he did the reverse, beginning his literary career at age 40 with publication of CANCER.

4.

Miller began the life he led in BIG SUR, California, USA, living in a shack, paying 5$ a month for the privilege. No electricity, plumbing, heat, or hot water. The nearest store 40 miles distant. He loved the area immediately, he tells us. Woke each morning blessing everything in sight. Found his unobtrusive neighbors helpful. Most of them worldly, many artists, others spiritual seekers. His affection for the place increases. A far cry, for him, from the "jungle life" of big cities, though primitive in the extreme. He recalls similar feelings of affection for the "grimy paradise" of his beloved Williamsburg (Brooklyn) childhood neighborhood. Within a couple of years he is living in a bigger place in Big Sur and with a wife and child. Able to buy the place with royalties paid him by his French publisher, money held in abeyance for years.

Miller begins his account of his life at Big Sur, BIG SUR AND THE ORANGES OF HIERONYMUS BOSCH, enumerating the paradisiacal qualities of the landscape. Thoreau-like in particularized evocation of the natural beauty. The flora, ocean (just outside the window), temperate climate...A paradise, in spite of rattlesnakes, weeds, gophers, buzzards, fog, rain, and pests, human and otherwise...Henry is sought out by misfits and vagabonds, regarding him as guru or source of aid, and, arriving unbidden, seeking an audience, or advice, or assistance, or to worship Miller, something he would not put up with (he would take a check though). Henry listens to some, offers to aid many—is rude or dismissive of others. Some become friends of Miller's. As do many of his neighbors, all of whom Miller finds special in some sense, even the ornery and the outlaws among them.

Miller is at his aphoristic best in this book. Not in the manner of Nietzsche's prophetic pronouncements; more like in Thoreau's quiet but authoritative manner. I offer a few: "One's destination is never a place but a new way of looking at things" (pg. 25). "The man who has seen the light follows the light" (pg. 28). "To feel the experience of aloneness is a spiritual achievement" (pg. 34).

Sketches of various neighbors and friends are given. Some funny and interesting; some too long, others boring because the reader does not know the people sketched, and in an encapsulation, no matter how great the writer—and there is no denying Miller is one of the greats ("a writer with the individuality of a giant"—Norman Mailer), it is not possible to make known the subject in much depth...

The woman whose house Miller purchased, is a Christian Scientist though with some ideas differing slightly from Mary Baker Eddy's (Miller calls Eddy "a great soul."). The woman is a source of spiritual succor to him, he reveals. She has seen the "light" (pg. 114), become a faith healer, an "instrument," Miller claims, working through, or in accordance with, a higher power or powers. Miller watches his friend rush to help others—rushing, in fact, "where angels fear to tread." He consuls refraining from intervention, developing a disinterested/interest in affairs of the world. Practicing "being" instead of "doing," and "only being," for "is it not the all?" (pg. 138) he asks. A question that leads us, readers, into the meat of Miller's new spiritual beliefs, his "blueprint," partially revealed in COLOSSUS.

The world, Miller states, does not need saving. Humankind might need saving, but that is a personal matter, a job for the individual to work at, and only the individual. No need to save the earth, Miller insists, because "abundance of the earth is inexhaustible" (pg. 140). "Do-gooders" and "fixer-uppers" he adds, do more damage than the carefree and "heedless sinners" (pg. 140). Those who fail to practice benign disinterest (the do-gooders) fail to tune in to harmony with "God, man, nature..." (pg. 140). The world needs no "fixing," he continues; "the world is, we are" (pg. 145). All is already fixed, he claims. "Everything created," he adds, "is also creative" (pg. 144), and all is in flux.

Give up, raise the flag of surrender, he advises. Embrace the angelic, which, is our true nature, ready to emerge whenever we get rid of self-will. We must step out of the unreality of the two worlds most of us live in: the world "we think we are in, and the world we would like to be in" (pg. 144).

Above all, recognize that the great problem of life, is not how to get along with your neighbors, but "how to get along with oneself" (pg. 145).

And if things should go wrong? (WHEN they go wrong, Miller says, assuredly), then get on your knees and pray! Not asking, begging, bartering, Miller cautions, but "living the thought—Thy Will Be Done!" (pg. 208).

Thus Miller's Buddhist, Christian, Hindu, Mystic, Anarchic, non-religion for the religious.

"to be an artist is a dog's life" (pg. 157)

Miller is patron saint to some writers, from the Big Sur area and elsewhere, because almost always generous with time and advice, help, hospitality, whatever...Miller sketches his experiences of dealing with some of them, laying down, along the way, some general rules, to those who will listen to rules: "if you can't give the is-ness of a thing, get the not-ness of it." Rejected? "Put your manuscript aside and write another and another and another." "Write in your own language...Deliver yourself, naked and vulnerable...Forego perfection...Accept the consequences which giving birth entails" (pg. 396).

A section of the book is devoted to the mail Miller receives and his reaction to it. The worst letters, he states, come from English men and women. He finds a "paucity of spirit" (pg. 145) in these communications. Making exceptions for "returned Welshman" John Cowper Powys, and English-poet-novelist Lawrence Durell. The latter a "master of prose style...pure and limpid," lines that "sing, bubble, effervesce..." (pg. 149). The former, though in his 80's, Miller hails, as his, Miller's, "youngest and gayest" correspondent. Letters from "gaseous vertebrates" Miller does not respond to. Most interesting, he states, are the letters received from "cranks, freaks, nuts, and plain lunatics" (pg. 151). To these, he might devote some time; might also devote time to the letters from foreign countries, Beruit, Java, India…

"the invigoration of sheer idleness" (pg. 102)

The work presents a home-y domesticated Henry Miller; relaxed, for the most part: a Dad, a neighbor, and advisor, counselor, confidante, and writer too, still at NEXUS, vol. 3 of THE ROSY CRUCIFIXION, a work he has struggled with for years, he reports, but one that, suddenly, when he picks it back up, starts to come together, and almost effortlessly, he relates. Big chunks of prose, the WORD coming to him, he insists, via the "Voice," an "it" dictating...As he stated in ASSASSINS, "we create nothing...it" does the creating. The "it" a change from previous implication of "God" in the process. Miller has only to listen, he claims, and the Voice feeds him the words he needs. As has happened to him previously, he reveals. Like while writing his study of D. H. Lawrence, when he heard the Voice speaking, and made some 800-plus pages of notes (but in mish-mash fashion and had to abandon the study. Some problem, with translation at the time, Miller implies). Another time, during his writing of TROPIC OF CAPRICORN, the Voice again began communicating, and so fast, Miller could barely keep up with it, he says. So insistent the Voice Miller carried a notebook and wrote while walking in the street, wrote while eating dinner, kept writing, obsessively, afraid the Voice would stop dictating "from the celestial recording room" (pg. 128, THE ORANGES OF…).

"life is being—art is making. Good life is the holy life (wholly living, wholly dying)"

All the familiar Millerite topics, interests, are herein included. Speaking of water-color painting, his painting, Miller says he started painting after seeing, in a store window in NYC, a group of prints of Turner's work, while previously, having seen a book of George Grosz's work, ECCE HOMO. These two events, plus his conversation about art with old pal Emil Schnellock, a successful commercial artist, inspired Miller to try his hand at art, despite the fact, or his belief, that he could not draw, or had ever shown any particular aptitude in the field.

During a sketch (this is a sketch-y book) of his "career" as artist, he comments that his best pieces are done when the thinking apparatus is turned off. When he approaches the act of painting without premeditated ideas about what he will create, or not, and then lets the fingers, the brush, take-over, the unconscious steps up and the hand, fingers, brush, pay fealty to it, and produce something "good" or interesting. Says he finds inspiration viewing the works of children and of the insane. Finds a naturalness in the work that is often missing in the celebrated artists, or professionals.

"in step but not in uniform" (pg. 207)

Miller is generally in fine fettle in this book. Joyous occasionally. Telling jokes in asides; playfully descriptive, delivering some laugh-out-loud comments, making innuendos and recording the comical banter between he and his children (two now, Val & Tony; Henry and his 3rd wife separated). Recording the coming and going of the kids, and writing a long section on his attempt to raise both children on his own. Or, not totally alone, for he recruits a writer friend to help out, the friend and Henry taking shifts in caring for the children. The section reads like a TV sitcom, 2 men and 2 kids. Who will win the battle? Henry, thinking of his childhood with his iron-maiden mother, refuses to discipline his kids, speaking rationally with them instead of scolding. A methodology that does not always work. Letting them go their own way, develop as they may, the kids run wild, develop in wrong directions, sometimes running over Henry in the process. The friend, coming to his wit's end, as does Henry, finally snaps and quits. Henry empathizes, and admits defeat also, too tired to continue with the job; he calls the wife to come and get the kids, and she does.

"to crave is only to pile up more karma"

Miller dabbles in metaphysics. Says there is a relation between right living and good fortune. Says fortune not good or bad, but either, depending on how we take it. By accepting our fate, our lot in life, we put ourselves in some kind of rhythm with higher laws, higher powers, "inscrutable laws of the universe" (very!), and good things often follow, "miracles" (pg. 217) even.

"Why?" is the forbidden question: asking it a "cosmic sabotage" (pg. 222). Penalized by the tribulations of Job (why me Lord? And the Lord answered: "why not you?").

This is the metaphysician speaking, Henry V. Miller, Professor Emeritus and Ad Infinitum of Whatsamattayou? The School of Great Truths. Miller quotes Kahlil Gibran, to buttress remarks made: Kablil writes, in effect, that because "universal life" (pg. 228) is so complex, deep, vast, etc., it makes history, hitherto written, seem like so much froth "on the surface of the sea of human life" (pg. 228).

Well. Let's hear it for the universe.

Detach! Miller urges. Dissolve it! (the problem). Ignore it. A studied indifference. Somewhat fatuously, Miller states that if your need is great enough it will be met. Met by the universe (yes, oh non-believer, the "universe") by the intelligence responsible for creation, or, "Mind that is the universe."

Continuing, in what could be called, loosely, a theological vein (or mystical) Miller states that the most potent continuous energy imaginable is "the will of God." Who God? The intelligence which governs the universe. Mind which is the universe. God is, simply, or not so simply, God. And the energy is something we can draw from IF we stop trying to run the show ourselves. It is our proud spirit that makes of us victims (think, Rimbaud). Dwell on the emptiness of things as well, Miller consuls, Buddhist-like. Sounding like a Chief Boo-Hoo in the Neo-American Church, Miller writes that "we pass from one state of dream to another." Sleep, wake, life, death. Sounding like Kabil Gilbran and Jonathan Livingston Seagull and the Mahatma of Fungol, Miller writes, "the imperishable soul" (pg. 29) is "vehicle in the eternal element of change" (transformation). Living and dying are one: all is one (good Buddhist). "Life is a very real dream from which there is no awakening" (pg. 28).

"star spangled Utopia of...deluded dipsy doodlers"

Miller becomes a bit long-winded in a somewhat superfluous screed on the shortcomings of Americans. The unhappiness behind the high standard of living. The moral bankruptcy, and stiflingly dull cultural life in America the Great. To say nothing of economic conditions, social inequities, etcetera, etcetera...The reader (this reader) begins to approach the Land of Nod, but then, Miller introduces Conrad Moricand into the narrative, the same astrologer whom Miller turned to during his, Miller's, Paris years (the two introduced via Anais Nin).

Moricand is a strange character; a dandy who tumbled in the world when duped out of his family fortune. Living in a Paris garret when Miller met him, but still fastidious of dress and deportment.

Miller had helped the poor guy out: small sums and cheery words. Then the war came and Miller bugged-out, first to Greece then America. And ended up living in a shack on Partington Ridge in Big Sur, California. Living with wife and child. This, 1946-7.

From out the blue, a letter from Moricand arrives. Reports he is still bad off; as bad if not worse than in Parisian and prewar days. In desperate straits, he tells Miller. And unless he, Miller, can help, he, Moricand, is "done for."

With forebodings (he should have heeded) Miller invites his old "friend" Conrad to Big Sur. To stay as long as he likes. Make himself at home. Miller clears out his studio, beside the shack, for Moricand to occupy.

Conrad arrives.

The first hint of trouble comes when Moricand requests of Henry that Henry buy some "Yardley" powder, because he, Moricand, "uses no other."

Following the perfume request, are requests for French cigarettes and some writing paper, cut in an unusual, non-standard size (Conrad uses "no other"). Requests Miller does his best to fulfill, but irked by the man's manner—Moricand's imperiousness. Henry makes a little speech to set his friend straight. Trying to induce a little gratitude, or at least appreciation, for what he, Miller, is doing—how he is putting himself out for his old "buddy." Tells Moricand that he is a free man, can come and go as he pleases, non? Reminds him of his former condition of miserableness, and that he, Henry, has rescued Moricand, from such. Oui?

Outside of the requests, Moricand is a good house guest, Miller states; one who keeps to himself, appearing only for meals. His presence, however, is upsetting to people who come to visit Miller, because of his "lunar, saturnian, and sepulchral" (pg. 307) mien. A "gloomy Gus" type. A Capricorn too, like Henry, but a Capricorn with an aura of death, and with "a bird of ill omen perched," Miller writes, "on his shoulder."

A week after his arrival, Moricand informs Henry that he is in need of a refill of his bottle of codeine. A drug he uses for sleep and for the pain caused him by a skin-condition—his legs are a "mass of sores" (pg. 309). Miller naively thinks he can walk into a drug store and buy the narcotic off the counter.

After informing Moricand of his, Miller's, failure to acquire the drug, Moricand says he will write his Swiss doctor and have it sent. Miller forbids Moricand to do so, knowing that he would be liable to prosecution were the authorities to uncover the illegal transaction.

One night Moricand asks Henry why he no longer seems interested in astrology. Henry replies that astrology was just another language for him to learn, and, besides, astrology deals in potentials, and he, Henry, is no longer interested in potential man, but in what a man actualizes, or realizes. Henry is for reality, he says. Does not deny the validity of astrology, but does not want, he continues, to become enslaved to "any one point of view" (pg. 320). Miller speculates that astrology came about at a time when humankind lost faith in itself, which is to say, lost wholeness. When humankind started to want to "know instead of be" (pg. 323)...Knowledge only weighs one down, Miller states. What the sum of knowledge, he asks: greater confusion, he answers. And not truth. Truth does not come from knowledge, he insists, but from surrender. Surrendering one's will and seeking the will of "IT."

"Call IT life, mind, God, whatever you please" (pg. 324).

Miller ends his peroration by recommending everyone learn to live "simply and wisely," meaning, forgetting, forgiving, renouncing, and abdicating.

Moricand isn't buying into Miller's spirituality. He shows Miller a package, from his, Moricand's, Swiss doctor: a refill of the codeine. Miller is furious (what did Miller expect?) and cannot forgive Moricand for endangering him, with the dope business, and going against his wishes. Cannot forgive Moricand either, for his, Moricand's, rudeness toward Miller's daughter (snatching a piece of bread from the girl, and with a "murderous" look). When Moricand tells Miller a story revealing himself as a pedophile, Miller views Moricand as "Satan himself."

Despite Miller's taking to task earlier the "fixer-uppers," he is something of a fixer himself. Trying to fix Moricand's life, an attempt Moricand cordially hates Miller for (no good deed goes unpunished!).

Realizing his folly, Miller thinks how "egotistical" (pg. 355) his attempt was, and tells himself "never again," and that he has learned his lesson.

Moricand, meanwhile, is feeling more desperate by the hour; feeling trapped in Big Sur and missing life of the city. He requests of Miller that Henry bring him to a hospital for treatment of the sores, now covering most of his body. Miller induces a friend to drive Moricand to town, where he undergoes a check-up by a hospital doctor who finds nothing organically wrong. "Hypersensitive, possible allergy," is the doc's finding. Miller sets-up Conrad in a hotel room (the hospital wants to do more tests) and then leaves, feeling great relief, and thinking that Moricand, and his pestilential itch, is off his, Henry's, hands.

The leave-taking does prove to be the last time Miller sees the man, but far from the last time Miller hears from him.

Moricand writes Miller from San Francisco asking for money. Miller complies then arranges, first a ship, then an airplane, to take Moricand back to Europe, but Moricand refuses to board either, and continues requests for more money. And if money not forthcoming, Moricand will expose, he says, Miller as a "traitor," and worse, to the authorities...A comedy of errors ensues, Miller referring to Moricand as "His Highness" or else, "Satanic Majesty." Moricand, through intervention of the Swiss consulate, finally does leave the county.

That is the end of the story, except for a postscript: a French newspaper Miller reads runs an obituary of Moricand, dead from heart attack while living in old age housing in Paris, 1954.

The Moricand story was published separate from THE ORANGES, as a novella titled "The Devil in Paradise." The story is among Miller's best.

5.

I have made mention previously of Miller's study of D. H. Lawrence, THE WORLD OF LAWRENCE, A Passionate Appreciation. The book written in the middle 1930's but not published until 1980 (Miller reading proofs the week before he died). Miller did not want the book published earlier, because, he said, it was a "mess."

He was right. "I got lost," Miller told Barbara Kraft, "I did not know what I thought" (pg. 89, HENRY MILLER, The Last Years). Also told her that while other of his books "flowed," (during the writing) the Lawrence book was written on "pure inspiration" (pg. 69, Kraft) his thoughts coming so fast he had trouble keeping up with them.

Lawrence is another of Miller's "spiritual brothers," like Rimbaud, Dostoevsky, Nietzsche, and Knut Hamsun. Miller calls the work "A Passionate Appreciation," to show his ardor for Lawrence and his work. The work and life of Lawrence provide Miller a jumping-off place to wade into his "mystical aesthetic" (pg. 239, Deerborn) in explications of theories on art, God, love, destiny, life...Inclusions, also, of writers from Petronius to Rimbaud; philosophers from Socrates to Spinoza; introduced at so fast a clip as to make one's head spin. And in prose often as turgid as a thicket, hard to see a way through, easy to get lost in...Abstruse in argument, sometimes unintelligible (to me). Miller often argues two contrary positions simultaneously, meanwhile achieving the stridency of a lawyer arguing a weak case.

Less inspiration, more organization, would have done the book good. Less sound and fury perhaps, could have, at least, signified something.

Miller likens the early Lawrence, writer of SONS & LOVERS, as an artist in the tradition of English letters, and being in union with nature, but the latter Lawrence, an "archangel flourishing a sword" (pg. 84), "evangel of a new order." Miller goes to great length to explicate the latter works, tracing, along the way, Lawrence's artistic and personal development.

Miller begins his appreciation by calling Lawrence a giant of literature, in a class with Shakespeare, Dante, and Goethe. Remarks that if, as Lawrence said, we are born "corpses," then he was the "most alive corpse" (pg. 38) ever. A heroic struggle, as artist, to write against the odds and illness (TB), but far less heroic in his struggle as a man. A titan as artist but often a "Chaplinesque figure" (pg. 40) as a human being. Miller calls Lawrence a true neurotic but, unlike a neurotic, a creator. Irrational, impossible; but a creative type par excellence, who wanted nothing less than to see a new man come to being. Lawrence's conflict with the world, a necessity, Miller posits, for his work.

In short, Lawrence a man of genius, also a monster. "Abnormal" as his critics said (but it is the abnormal man/woman who "widens the frontiers of life" for the rest of us, Miller writes).

Lawrence is "sex-crucified, sex-sodden," Miller writes: This was his demon, his personality. Lawrence was in love with himself, Miller opines; thought himself a god, and had a distinct inability to be human, or natural, or to live with others on any close terms. He is all that a monster could be, but besides this incidental biographical fact, he was also someone who refused to be broken by the world. As one of his character's remarks (AARON'S ROD), "face everything...break the old forms...never let our own pride and courage of life be broken" (pg. 76). Remarks that strike to the heart of the Henry Miller persona, which is always "happy and gay," enjoying oneself even in the midst of defeat, because to do otherwise is to admit defeat. An impossible admission.

This Lawrentian intransigence leads Miller to a discussion of the mystic, the one who admits to no heaven but the here and now; the one who accepts—who lets things be as they are, and is whatever he/she is; one who is nourished by everything, pain, joy, war, peace...One, in other words, who lives in the Kingdom of Heaven. Who takes possession of him/herself, and by so doing possesses the world. And who thus becomes, through supreme identification with life, the symbol of life...Becomes another "Henry Miller" or, a D. H. Lawrence.

Modern life is a sickness because man/woman is no longer "whole." There has been a split and dissolution of the soul—as a dissolution of the macrocosm: a schizophrenia has resulted. In this sick state of the world, Joyce and Proust, as representative authors, illustrate, in their works, the sorry state the soul is in. Both reject the soul for Mind (unlike Dostoevsky, who, as a "man of God," wrote of nothing but the soul).

Joyce and Proust have created epics, but sick ones, Miller posits. Analysis and portrayals of disintegration, mirrors of the sick mind of modern humankind. In Proust, "a deterioration of the heroic" (pg. 106) occurs, writes Miller, and in Joyce a "deformity of vision." Both are "defeatists" who escape reality into the "world of art."

Writing more of a diatribe than criticism, Miller bemoans the fact, as he sees the facts, that there are no more creative men left in the world, only worms, like critics, psychoanalysts, statisticians...Non-creative worms of modern times who feed on the dead and near-dead, rather than themselves creating...

All the modern sickness presaged in Shakespeare, Miller states, in the sick mind of Hamlet.

There is no "demonic quality' (pg. 117) in Proust either, Miller writes, and no genuine madness in the artists of modern times, only "neuroticism" (pg. 115). The Surrealists envy, in their minds, the criminal, the insane, the sexually depraved, but the Surrealists themselves do not go crazy, do not really live, Miller implies, because they too are sick with the modern-mind disease, which the work of Joyce best represents. His "luxuriant" (pg. 116) language, Miller writes, not a sign of "new life or vitality, but the manifestation of a cancer" (pg. 116). The modern illness a case of instinct turned in upon itself. A preponderance of Mind, as opposed to body or Soul...

Lawrence, like Rimbaud, is a "prophet, seer, visionary" (pg. 112). A "Savior," even, in his frenzied moments. And aware, supremely so, that death is upon "us" from cradle to the grave. And spending his life, Miller says, crying out against death, in anguish and despair, crying for "life! Life everlasting!" (pg. 117) Like the sage Henry V.

Miller, the courtly misogynist, analyzes Lawrence's presumed hatred of women. The idea being that Lawrence, like most of us, men and women, was stuck in the womb, imprisoned there by an excess of his mother's love. Was not truly born but contained in the clutching womb. How to escape? A mighty effort involved, helped by the death of his mother. From the "embryonic" stage he is freed, and becomes himself, "at last!" But remains, Miller claims, "a cripple" of sorts because he, Lawrence, had not freed himself of his own accord, but was "simply released" (pg. 121) by his mother's death. His emotional deformity is behind his attack upon the world; his revolt a result of his lack of "wholeness." He projects and universalizes this conflict in his works. And never did achieve "individuation" (pg. 234, THE BOOKS IN MY LIFE, Henry Miller).

Seeking wholeness through sex, but not finding it, Lawrence continues to revolt, but now against his wife and the "comforting annihilation of her big womb" (pg. 127).

Revolts even against the gods too, not realizing that, in Miller's cosmogony, he, Lawrence, is already a god—as is everyone who has found their god-nature. We are born angels, but have forgotten that fact, Miller claims, or else purposely ignore it. God is an "absolute" Miller writes, which we all create in order to deal with our "irrational fear of death" (pg. 124). An illusion, of course (and all that is built on illusion "must crumble and be rebuilt," pg. 124). Thus, gods appear and disappear "ad infinitum" (pg. 124).)

Lawrence remains in conflict between his human and divine self, Miller says;

like Jesus, Lawrence is also a world-saver, an idealist who, confronted with reality, becomes "rebel, revolutionist, and advocate of violence" (pg. 123). Like Jesus, Miller says, who also advocated violence ("I come with a sword.") Types, these world-savers, who alternate, Miller posits, between the comic and the tragic. Their reactions to life, to even trifles, are not as others react; they make everything symbolic as well as personal, which, in turn, reinforces their role as gods—keeps them as "one against the many," which, in Lawrence's case, fed a persecution complex. He needed to be despised (because, Miller writes, the thought that it, the world, might love him, was too horrible to contemplate).

This savior-type is cracked; he/she is one who, "unable to conquer his personal division, arranges the world in terms of it" (pg. 126). A male of this type has an "unusual portion of femininity"—the feminine becomes his spiritual side. Many are the similarities between this type and the artist, Miller states. The savior-type as artist (Lawrence) with an abnormal mix of male/female, has, as artistic goal, to "recreate his personality" (pg. 126). An evolution, Miller remarks, that, eventually, leads him to "godhood" (Jesus sacrificed himself in order to become whole, Miller opines—as man he joins with God, and the Father and he, Jesus, become one).

In Lawrence, the attempt at an integrated personality met with failure in the sex realm and also in the friendship realm; and his frustration, consequently, grew in proportion to his failures. He came to realization that what he, Lawrence, really wanted, was to establish himself as "leader." That, if he could not find God, he would become one. Thus, does Lawrence "skirt insanity" (pg. 127).

Returning, after a great circumlocution, we see that Lawrence's misogyny is predicated upon his split personality, the bi-sexual character of his make-up, which, according to Miller, Lawrence refused to recognize. Lawrence mistakenly attributed the animal nature of man, to woman, and the spiritual nature of woman, to man.

Being a "leader" for Lawrence is belonging to a natural "aristocracy," an "aristocrat of the spirit," and receiving the "divine rights" (pg. 131) that go with the notion. Like a little King, in a way. If only he could make his subjects—like his wife—respect his authority!

Using Lawrence's case—his growth as artist and struggles as a man—Miller makes some general remarks on artists and creation. Says that an artist's work—poem, novel, film, painting, etc., is his/her only expression of wholeness. Otherwise, in between acts of creation, there exists the fragmented self, trying to return to the womb, fighting (with oneself) the Oedipal complex (Lawrence a great sufferer of) and living as a human being, like other humans, only with the distinction that the non-artists do not get to live in the flame of the Holy Ghost, which is what happens, to Lawrence, and to Miller (who I assume to be speaking of himself as well) when in the throes of creation.

How to break free of the "ideological mask of culture" (pg. 142) and from history itself? How to sever the umbilical cord that holds us in place? How to bring on a new type of human being? One way is through friendship, Miller, who always seemed to have a load of friends, seems to be saying. Lawrence tried this route, but failed, and wound up friendless after he cast off his only male companion, Murry, as not up to snuff. Claiming Murry to be incapable of knowing him, Lawrence, Murry is told off, thus does Lawrence, Miller writes, lose his one human friendship and then begins, in his isolation, making friends of the great spirits of the past...An artist looks for a friend, Miller states, who is an image of his/her self. In Lawrence's case, a narcissistic split-personality schizoid type. No wonder Murry did not fit the bill. Proust failed too (but Proust was an "invert" Miller writes, with a different set of problems). Failing friendship, Lawrence tried to become a leader, so that he could show others how to be, change them, and thus, make of them possible friends...A screwy notion, and one that did not work for Lawrence, Miller states.

Sounding like his spiritual brother Rimbaud, Miller says that madness and hallucination are necessary if a new cultural order is to arise. A need for "manic personalities" (pg. 148). This new artist-type must, Miller states, give the world not only his/her work but self as well. Must devour him or herself for the sake of the world. So that the creative-types' deaths will nourish the soil (spiritual soil). By taking "root" and devouring, the artist returns, somehow, to his/ her natural self, and in turn—the enchanted process gives back "life to God."

Back to the Savior type, of which, Lawrence belongs. The "schizophrenic type par excellence" (pg. 152). Split, inwardly, and because unable to cure himself, trying to save the world to resolve his inward conflict. As noted earlier, Lawrence failed to solve his problems, became God, a power unto himself, and tried to assert authority over those about him, and putatively, the world. But it was lonely being God. He became an unhappy Caesar, and stepped down from his throne and joined the people, though still a "spiritual aristocrat." Instead of following in the steps of Christ, Buddha, Mahomet, Lawrence became an artist, believing he could use art to change the world. Instead of stressing the religious, he stresses the dark animal side of existence, and announces a belief in the blood, the flesh, as being wiser than the intellect (later Fascists took note). Following which, Miller writes, Lawrence established as symbol of the conflicting human spirit, the dark god, Quetzalcoatl, in his novel THE PLUMED SERPENT.

Now, like Nietzsche, Lawrence begins to smash, with a spiritual hammer, the old idols, symbols, icons, all those "dead letters" (pg. 156) of the law. A new reality comes into being, the reality of the artist, which has "its roots" Miller states, "in conflict" (pg. 156).

By the long arduous process of turning him or herself into a god, the artist has a chance to sway the great masses by giving the people, new symbols to stare at, symbols that are meaningful, unlike the old symbols. Through the change, the artist can thwart or alter destiny. He/she is the ultimate game changer. This is, Miller states, how the Dionysian-type works his/her magic, his/her destruction, and his/her death—the dying over and over to achieve, finally, insight and life, more life…

From Lawrence Miller swings to discussion of Nietzsche and thence to Spengler, Havelock Ellis, Otto Rank, Copernicus, and Einstein, all in consideration of Faustian culture—which rose after the Renaissance. A culture marked by neurosis, and endemic fear. "Fear of extinction, which is driving us to extinction" (pg. 165). The fear a symptom of the deeper cultural malaise of despair, failure, and emptiness.

According to Lawrence, the ancient world was entirely religious AND godless. Not until the individual began to feel separated (from the tribe) and ate from the Tree of Knowledge, did the conception of a god arise. The cosmos, to ancient people, always was, like a fact, and therefore needed no god to explain it; it was itself god and divine and the origin.

Miller applauds this anti-scientific interpretation, a fictive and metaphysical, creative and poetic approach, as explanation of the universe—deciphering of "the rude hieroglyph of life" (pg. 169). Artists, if attuned to the nature of changing phenomena, and standing outside all systems of thought (not joining, simply apprehending) give a truer version of reality than science, Miller states.

Still on artists, Miller says the great catastrophe for the artist is to lose vision. One way that occurs is if the artist joins, becomes one of either the "freak categories" (pg. 171), charlatan, criminal, lunatic; or one of the human roles, "montebank, murderer, redeemer" (pg. 171). Such moments of human weakness, as the artist might show, are met by the mob, "waiting for that weakness," (pg. 171) in order to crucify.

Lawrence was the "last man of genius" to write in the English language, Miller states, and his work points to the future. To people who consider Lawrence's work too difficult, too layered, too odd, Miller suggests that the problem of comprehension lies not with the work but with the modern age, an age of neurosis, which cannot comprehend Lawrence. This comprehension, Miller states, awaits an "age again of men" (pg. 174).

In Miller's view, LADY CHATTERLY'S LOVER lacks the "substance of Lawrence's gospel" (pg. 175) and thus is less than top-shelf. The book a "genital banquet" (pg. 175) in which Lawrence's mysticism is implicit rather than explicit. The book a failure, because, in Miller's view, outside of its obscenity—which Miller understands as example of healthiness (as it was for ancient people), the rest is but padding for mass consumption. And yet, in the novel, Lawrence came nearest to the whole man, Miller claims. A man who "can live in the world and accept it too" (pg. 177). A man not only of spiritual nature but one who uses the old John Thomas as well. Unlike Christ, Miller notes, who went about without cock or balls, a situation rectified by Lawrence, Miller says, in his, Lawrence's, book, THE MAN WHO DIED, a story of a non-self-castrated Christ.

If sex is the starting point and goal, Lawrence asks, as well as end point, what is beyond? And answers: beyond is death. Only death.

Woman creates man in her womb and pushes him out so that man can act like man: build cities, civilization, religions, architecture, all to sustain the "illusion of his necessity" (pg. 182). Woman knows man is unnecessary—she tolerates him; she created him, not unselfishly, but to have a larger life herself.

When Christ came along, he preached a love that went beyond any "ordinary" love, Miller posits; he preached a "cruel love that overlooked woman entirely" (pg. 184).

The masculine world (see above) is, in modern days, being appropriated by woman, Miller states. She, like a "black widow spider" (pg. 181) has paralyzed man and invaded the arena of masculinity. A perversion in the maternal instinct has resulted, Miller says. The role of man and woman, which, to Miller, is an antagonistic one—a war even—is being reversed, or sacrificed, in the name of equality of the sexes, meaning, to Miller, total distortion of the roles of each. The woman is "fecundator," her world built on "flux, a living and dying, a birth and death, a metamorphosis" (pg. 185)...Man is a moral, religious, code-maker, and law-giver; woman is "amoral...uncivilizing...and destructive ("in the sense that all creation is destructive" pg. 185).

The struggle between man and woman, the modern usurpation by woman of man's prerogatives, was given voice in the plays of Ibsen and Strindberg, Miller notes. But Strindberg, in particular, was a misogynist, whereas Lawrence, because of his latent femininity, arrived at a "deeper understanding" (pg. 188) of the conflict.

The problem of the distortion of sexual relations is, according to Miller, the exhaustion of the Christian ideal and its "evil seeds." An ideal that Lawrence wars against, and tries to put himself "beyond the sexual view of religion" by restoring the dark cruel primitive male god Queztalcoatl.

Joyce, on the other hand, expresses only hatred of woman, through his "primitive Christian attitude" (pg. 188), stressing only the carnal side of woman and in turn exalting the "spiritual generative principle of the male" (pg. 188). Molly Bloom's lubricity and obscenity is case in point. Joyce's hatred of his mother, and of the church's indifference, is an "admission" (pg. 188), Miller writes, of defeat at woman's hands...Not so with Lawrence, who "emancipated" himself. And thus does not seek solution to life IN love, but THROUGH love" (pg. 189). Lawrence's "sex mysticism" was his effort, Miller writes, to "give back to sexuality its cosmic character" (pg. 190).

It was Lawrence's idea to place the emphasis on the man, salvation through the self, through the creation of a higher, fanatical, Utopist idea, in accord with the wisdom of the best minds. But Lawrence did not have enough stamina for rigorous development of his idea, Miller writes. But his spiritual revolt, Miller argues, did show the way, in that his effort to have done with "idealism, moralities, and democracy" (pg. 191) brought him to the body, the Sacred Body, which, to him, meant that salvation could be found not only in mind, religion, idea, education, etc., but in body too, which "means action," Lawrence wrote, "and action is a refuge...and it is precisely this refuge that the "new humanism' seeks" (pg. 192). Thus Lawrence's sensuality rather than sexuality. Sensuality means animal instinct; sexuality "a false cultural attitude" (pg. 192) and "a narrow interpretation of life" (pg. 192). Lawrence did not believe, Miller claims, in just simply "Greek revival of body culture" either, but that, through integration of personality, and recognition of the body, as center of a "mystic humanism," a "mystic union of the universe" might be achieved.

Lawrence distrusted the mind, feared the mind, Miller writes, because it was "the court of death" (pg. 192) for the instincts. Mind must give way to the blood, for though mind may offer the most fantastic thoughts, it is the body that is anchored, and "all forms of thought," Miller writes, "are fixed therein" (pg. 195), in "the mystic fundament of the body" (pg. 195), writes Miller, somewhat mystifyingly. During the Renaissance, Miller continues, the body came into its own, but in Shakespeare's England it had deteriorated, and from Shakespeare on, following the "lovely and fearless" (pg. 196) Chaucer, the canker of doubt poisoned Western humankind. That doubt expressed through Hamlet. The great Faustian soul ran smack into Hamlet and doubt created a "Hamlet-Faustian antagonism" (pg. 195).

How and why did this mind/body split happen? Lawrence supplies answer: "syphilis." People became cold to one another, in dread of the "pox." A dread of everything developed, except "ideas."

Hamlet is "syphilis," Miller announces, "the syphilis of the mind" (pg. 197). A disease that struck at Lawrence's "blood consciousness" (pg. 197) Miller notes. Miller suggests the possibility of the plagues of the 14th through 17th centuries in Europe as the "outward manifestation of the inward devastation of Western man's soul" (and we thought it a bacillus!).

People of the Middle-Ages were integrated, Miller asserts, but from the Reformation onward there is an increasing divorce of soul from mind. Leading to the exaltation of the latter, and then the bankruptcy of the mind and consequent paralysis of the instincts. Leading to the modern day dilemma which Lawrence tried to alter, his language being, Miller claims, "joy of the body recovering its soul" (pg. 198).

Lawrence's effort to recreate humankind was an impossible job, Miller opines. Which Lawrence knew, and the reason why he rose to such fury and passion, in his work. "Fulminat(ed) in a bacteriological stew of dream and frenzy" (pg. 198), and called for death—spiritual death of the race, so that a new race could take over…

"A man of spirit," (pg. 200) Miller refers to Lawrence. Who emphasized, during his shortened life (44 years), the instinct, blood-consciousness, the solar plexus...The last of the three stressed by Miller in his own work—work he claimed written not from the head but from the gut. A man who also glorified the animal nature, Miller adds, speaking of Lawrence (unlike Dostoevsky, who glorified solely spirit—though both "wrestled with God" pg. 205).

Miller writes that, in modern man, the fear of older humankind has been replaced by a Fear of Life, which, in turn, creates an "empire of neurosis" (pg. 215), ever present to modern imagination. The effect of this fear has turned art to "compensatory, substitutive, escapism" (pg. 215). No longer able to approach things, or life, spiritually, because no longer in touch with spirit, present day humans approach spiritual problems via scientific jargon. Coincident with the fear is, Miller posits, a growing terror of reality, which, is death...Slacking on the life impulse, humankind loses the fear of death (that is, his/her urge for immortality) which, in turn, leaves no raison d'etre for the artist, unless a new religion or new personality should come to being. Which is impossible, Miller says, because we are soulless, rootless, and myth-less, and dead besides, "killed by the intellect's triumph over the soul" (pg. 210).

A fine how-do-you-do. Totally screwed—or are we? We still can reclaim, Miller writes, the "illusion of imperishability" (pg. 216).

Some say wisdom is the hope but Miller denies this route, claiming our mentality precludes such development: our ideologies, deities, and mores against us. Besides, wisdom, once the role of the artist, is now granted the sage, and the sage is the analyst (which, in Miller's view, means "stagnation" pg. 220). A Renaissance is possible, he concedes, but that depends upon the artists of the future. Needed are artists like Nietzsche, who rescued thought from the philosophers by the "force of his artistic endowment" (pg. 217), and Lawrence, who "rescued art from the psychologists through his religious endowment" (pg. 217). The future artists may, by some miracle, resurrect a new body, spirit, and culture. Restore, as "Orphic artists" (pg. 218) a "magic sense, magic relation with the people, the mass, the herd." A restoration, Miller goes on to say, difficult in the extreme because an era of "collectivity" has set in, and the collective spells death for individual artists.

Lawrence is one such Orphic artist, Miller opines. Tried to restore men their faith by "giving impulse and direction to their living" (pg. 222). Lawrence, in comparison with Joyce and Proust, was an "Apostle of Day" to their "slaves of Night" (pg. 222). Lawrence tried to bring people back to the source, heart of the cosmos, by use of a "mystic labyrinth of symbols and metaphor" (pg. 222). A yearning for the impossible, which is, I suspect, what makes Lawrence such an exemplar and hence of such interest to Miller...Trying to remain human, Lawrence's demon drove him mad. Seeing, expressing, the futility and frustration of life, Lawrence continued his vision quest and made public his mystical unions, becoming one with the universe, then dissolving. He tried to communicate what he experienced, but it was an impossible task, incommunicable, Miller states, because each must experience the quest for him or herself...Not only artist, but prophet, Miller says of Lawrence, and visionary, his works a record of his quest-experiences, a diary of sorts, recording each new growth, and subsequent disillusionment, in each new book..."A creative suicide," is Miller's final opinion on Lawrence. Whose death was a "climax in the progression towards new being" (pg. 231). A failure—a "terribly human failure" (pg. 237)—in his attempt to express the ineffable, but a grand and great "failure" who "triumphed by giving expression to his failure" (pg. 237).

ADDENDUM

I have decided to discuss Miller's seminal book, TROPIC OF CANCER, last. Mainly because in the book are all of Miller's concerns, his stock in trade as a writer, the last and first words on his pet subjects, his "philosophy," if you will. The work is his opus, the one book of his in which form and substance share the spotlight—are equally of concern to the author. CANCER begins in journal form, "an assemblage" (Ferguson, pg. 181) but quickly coalesces into a tight narrative as episodes dominate and personalities begin to take over the book. The main personality that of the author, or rather, the persona, of an insouciant, accommodating, irrepressible, and vital, "Henry Miller." (Note the quotation marks—I want to remind readers that the book presents a persona, not necessarily the "real" Henry Miller, the 5 foot 8 inch double-crowned hooded-eyed former resident of Brooklyn's 14th ward.) A persona that has "true good will," writes Barbara Kraft (HENRY MILLER, The Last Days, pg. 15) "impossible in reading not to like him, not to feel exuberant, to enter into the experience of the senses..."

CANCER is a book about Death, or rather, expostulation of a philosophy, so-called, The Universe of Death. The necessity of death, in life, so that, as Erica Jong writes (THE DEVIL AT LARGE, pg. 100), "man can begin to live in the spirit." CANCER was written in 1932 and published, in France, in 1934. Four drafts of the book done between 1932-34. An early title of the book was I SING THE EQUATOR (pg. 153, Deerborn). Chunks of CANCER were said to have been transferred from Miller's letters to Emil Schnellock, Miller's childhood artist-friend, into the manuscript. Barbara Kraft called CANCER "a poet's book." It is that—and more.

Henry Miller in the process of being. Torn from the womb, through the intervention of Paris. Paris the "instrument" that tears the embryo from the womb. Henry Miller is the embryo; he is mother also, big with the book he is writing—The Last Book! Germinating in his belly.

The Universe of Death is correlative of the "Enormous Womb," an essay Miller wrote, as satire, and published in "The Booster," a golf-club production run as a lark, for two issues, by Miller, Alfred Perles, and the rest of the Villa Seurat crowd. The imprisoning womb that keeps us from being our true selves—keeps us in bondage through its clutching, and when we fail to break free, remain people sundered at birth, split, or double-split (like D. H. Lawrence), unable to integrate our personalities and thereby fail to navigate successfully in the world. Frustrated by life's demands, which, in turn, causes acute suffering on our part. The womb was safety and security: all attempts to reenter are insufficient and only exacerbate our insecurity, anxiety, angst, ennui...Afflictions that, consequently, cause neurosis.

Born dead! D. H. Lawrence posited (pg. 117, THE WORLD OF LAWRENCE, Henry Miller). "Born a corpse, and stuck inside a tomb...Specters and ghosts, shadows; we are not solid...Do not live in the flesh...Our instincts and intuitions are dead."

Henry Miller lives at the Villa Borghese, where all are dead, or dying, or about to die; that is, cast into a dead universe. The Universe of Death. And still attached to the clawing womb. And doomed to remain dead unless somehow able to detach from the womb, break its clutching grip, and integrate the personality, thus breaking the fetters that hold him, and us, back. Either escape, or get in step, lock-step, and march "toward the prison of death!" (pg. 1).

Henry Miller, in his 2nd year since moving to Paris. Living now at the Villa Borghese. With Boris, who owns the place, and is the Big Cheese. And with Boris's wife, a "dried up cow," and with Elsa, the maid. Boris (real name, Michael Fraenkel) is in process of selling the place. Henry has his bags packed. Ready to vacate at a moment's notice: ready to go back out to the streets, where people are making a mess of their lives—everyone with a private tragedy. The tragedy that is in the blood of the times, along with "misfortune, ennui, grief, suicide" (pg. 11). An atmosphere saturated with disaster, frustration, and futility. A fact, or facts, that do not particularly bother our narrator, H. M., who enjoys the tragedies, little and big. Cries for more of them, bigger disasters, greater failures! Fuck a duck!

Boris is a writer who glows with a flame, possessed. Carl, another writer, also glows, but Carl (real name, Alfred Perles) is also a "prick," Henry says, an "aristocrat...who lives in a dementia praecox kingdom all his own" (pg. 45). There is Sylvester too, who will never be a writer, Henry says, not even should Sylvester's plays become Broadway hits...Sylvester (real name, Joe Schrank) is married to Tania (Bertha Schrank). Tania the desirable! Henry is in love with her and writes her novella-sized letters...Carves her initials into the nail of his big toe...

Moldorf is a writer too; he is also God. As all are gods. As all are divine. Those aware of their angelic nature, become the gods they, and we, were meant to be, that they, and we, once were, in ancient annals of time immemorial...God or not-God, everyone is dead at the Villa and elsewhere. A Universe of Death! Born into it. A world "reducing to zero" (pg. 223) and "tottering...crumbling...used up and polished like a leper's skull" (pg. 234).

"You and I, we were born corpses, and we are corpses...We are inside the tomb, and the tomb is wide and shadowy...We walk and talk, wrapped in our winding sheets, all the time wrapped in our winding sheets"(quote from Lawrence, pg. 117, THE WORLD OF LAWRENCE).

After the Villa Borghese it is a bench in a cinema for Henry. Compliments of his Russian friend, Eugene. A page later he has shifted quarters to a mattress on the floor of another Russian's apartment. For one night only though, because the mattress "saturated with embalming fluid" (pg. 65). From the mattress to the apartment of Nanantatee, a Hindu pearl merchant, aka "Mister Non-Entity." "A crazy duck," Miller calls him, with a crippled arm, who calls Henry "Enhree." "Now you will sweep the floor please, Enhree..." The merchant becomes comic foil for a wonderfully funny scene. One that leads to the episode in a brothel featuring a Hindu boy—one of Gandhi's men...Brought to the brothel by Henry, who is escorting the boy around town (per Nanantatee's request). The boy, mistaking the bidet for a toilet, drops two enormous turds into the water. Causing a big scene, featuring an irate Madame...Afterward, inconsequential to the event, Henry goes into a sort of swoon, and realizes that there is no injustice "on the meridian of time" (pg. 88), only the "poetry of motion" that creates an illusion of truth and drama. A fact, as Henry sees it, and something humankind will endure—war, crime, poverty, etc., to escape acknowledging. The hideous dung-heap of reality must be avoided at all cost. That humankind is, basically, screwed from the start, is a fact, but, why let a little thing like that, thinks Henry, get in the way of a good time?

With history meaningless—has all the wars and revolutions altered in one iota humankind's nature? Miller asks—and at the extremity of his endurance, Miller goes forward, forward to devour, he says, and like a hungry hyena. Forward to fatten up! No longer trying to save himself, the little bit of meat left on his bones—fuck that! Henceforth, he moves forward as a savage, spiritually dead, but physically alive, and morally free…

CAPRICORN was the Land of Fuck. CANCER is the Kingdom of Cunt. Van Norden the knight of the realm, a walking cock. A newspaper man of Henry's acquaintance, and "cunt-struck" victim of his own psyche, Van Norden (real name, Wambly Bald) spends much of his life chasing the female, like an opium addict his fix. And without knowing why. Uses them, the women, to forget himself, he tells Henry. The women give him, Van Norden, a "good feeling," he continues, making him feel "sort of spiritual-like..." (pg. 117).

Henry thinks Van Norden a little mad. Van Norden is in the prison of himself, Henry thinks: being alone, his greatest fear. Van Norden says he dislikes himself, and can't express himself; admits that he is an "egotist," but not selfish, he tells Henry. Not like Carl, that "little prick," Van Norden says. ("Prick" because, we learn shortly, Carl has a rich "cunt" on the line and will not let Van Norden in on it—will not even tell her name.) Van Norden tells Henry, that, one day, he, Van Norden, will lay down on the operating table and expose his guts...Write the great book…

Which, is exactly what Henry Miller is doing!

Henry is callous toward death and dying. Seems so anyway. "Corpses mangled...lay thick in the street," he quotes from an unnamed text. Then comments, "lovely book! Refreshing!" (pg. 37). This is not really callousness, but affirmation, in line with the "philosophy" of The Universe of Death, which is a recognition, or acknowledgment, that death is a fact of existence—one of, in fact, the prominent facts in its importance in the life, psychic, and physical, of humankind. "Death is neither here nor there. Death is a temporal, relative fact" (pg. 142, THE WORLD OF LAWRENCE). Why deny it? Why try and keep mum about it. Make a secret of it? Why should it not, the fact of it, be celebrated even? Death is. We are. Let the truth rule...Not a philosophy for the squeamish.

An "anarch" (Miller's word) wading through the squalor of Paris streets leprous with a fetid odor, "with sex running through like a sewer" (pg. 38), during a "poisonous malefic spring" (pg. 38). Skirting the approaches of prostitutes, who attach themselves "like barnacles" (pg. 142), although making the acquaintance of two: Germain and Claud. Claud, whom Henry feels a "genuine affection for," has a soul, Henry says, and a conscience, plus refinement, which, he remarks, "is bad—in a whore" (pg. 41). Germain is not refined; she is "a whore all the way through" (pg. 41). Someone who enjoys her role, is satisfied; and has a "good heart" too, Miller remarks, but then writes: "a whore's heart...Not really good, but lazy, indifferent..." (pg. 41). The whores and their "maquereaus" part of the décor of Montmartre. So are the tourists. From whom Van Norden finds his girlfriends. Especially from the females of America. "They come over here to get laid," he tells Henry. "They're dying for it" (pg. 93). And are superior to the French girls, Van Norden opines, because all the French girls want is money or else to marry-up...

The streets were different when Miller had no money, no friends, and nowhere to live. Bereft of all his possessions and spending days, and nights, wandering. Snoozing on park benches. Trying to stay clear of cops. Standing with his hand out, under the "Tout va bien" signs. Belly gnawing with hunger, and starting to see strange things, recognizing trifles as omens, portents...Like Strindberg, in his madness, Henry thinks...Splotches of blood in a muddy lane fill Henry with a sense of foreboding. He sees his blood spilled: the day shatters in hallucination. All the mirrors are cracked. People begin to look like demons. The streets speak of loneliness, yearning, and failure. Cruel streets, of ghoulish lamp posts, buildings that remind one of prisons, or else torture chambers...Buildings that stare through empty black eyes... A scarlet sunset like blood, more murderous than beautiful, more obscene than lovely. Then, "black night, like frozen fat in a soup tureen" (pg. 218).

The streets had a different aura then. Not so happy or gay. With a particular angoisse.

After the Englishman Peckover, a proofreader for the newspaper, falls down an elevator shaft and dies, Henry gets his job. Being a proofreader, Miller remarks, is a little like being God. "In the world but not of it" (pg. 133). The calamities of life pass under Henry's nose, but move him not. All he cares about is orthography and punctuation. Murders, rapes, wars, disasters big or small, leave him cold. He only heats up over semi-colons, and parentheses.

Miller's American friends are baffled over his obvious joy in living: why he isn't as miserable as they are. Does he really like it "over here?" they ask. To which he replies, a resounding "oui!"

"A world without hope but no despair," is Miller's credo. Like a "new religion," he remarks. He is content; cannot imagine what he would gain if he were to be named editor of the paper, or even President of the United States. A return to America? For what? So he can get in harness again? Work like a mule to buy things he has no need of, does not want? Bah! In Europe, he comments, everyone is potentially a zero. Should anyone become something out of the ordinary, it is considered either an accident or a miracle. In America, he reflects, everyone is potentially Presidential timber. Everyone gets a firecracker stuffed up their ass to give them pep and go-getterism...He is content where he is, he tells his friends. He likes the place. Is happy with himself. Happy, elated, not to be any longer in New York! Does not even think of America; tries not to think of Mona, his wife of seven years duration, either...in New York. Thinking of her, it tears him to pieces...Makes him feel like he is falling into an abyss...

The genito-urinary system is in process of dissolution. Earth is moving out its orbit, its axis shifted. Snow from the North drifting, heralding a new ice age. The fetal world dying, "turning to dead mastoid" (pg. 148). Transverse sutures closing up; deltas drying out; river beds smooth as glass, and the drains "clogged with strangled embryos" (pg. 147). Only the artists are holding their own. Matisse, for example. Remains at the core and "solidly fixed" (pg. 148). He who transforms the "negative reality of life" (pg. 146) into art (like Proust did). And in his painting, the human flesh "expresses the miracle of breathing" (pg. 147), and refuses the "consummation of death." Matisse has escaped the death in life Lawrence spoke of. Has worked his way into life through a long arduous process of integration of personality. (See previous chapter.)

After Henry loses his job on the newspaper (economy measure) he starts hanging around artists' studios, getting to know people, and trying to stave off hunger. In this milieu he meets an American dilettante who is to assume a prominent part in the last third of CANCER. Fillmore (real name, Richard Osborn), is a young man in the diplomatic service, and from a rich family. Fillmore is "slumming" while having a good time and hoping to be thought a bohemian artist. He impulsively invites Miller to move into his studio/apartment and act as companion. Miller likes Fillmore for his adventurous spirit. Plus Fillmore is generous, and picks up the tab. Also leaves Henry ten francs each morning.

Things go "smoothly," Henry reports, until Fillmore invites a "dame" to live in the apartment. A Russian, and Princess to boot, who speaks four languages. But has the clap.

Fillmore has bronchitis. Henry has piles. The princess can't fuck; Fillmore can't talk; Henry can't sit. Fillmore and Princess lie in bed together like brother and sister. Henry lies on a cot next to the stove. He thinks of Whitman, the "greatest writer America has produced." The only great writer, according to Henry. After Whitman, there is nothing more to be said about American literature. "The poet of body and soul...The first and last poet" (pg. 217). A "MAN" Miller writes. "A free healthy spirit" (pg. 217). (An "invert" too, as Miller labeled Proust, but no mention of that...) From Whitman, his thoughts go to other artists, whose task, he writes, is to "overthrow existing values" (pg. 228), and make order from chaos, also sow strife and ferment so that "by emotional release those who are dead may be restored to life" (pg. 228). Artists must go the whole hog, he opines. Like Dostoevsky, who "went the whole gamut...abyss to the stars" (pg. 230). Going whole hog means, or could mean, tearing one's hair out, bellowing (in or outdoors, I presume), and, like the beasts, ripping and goring, if need be...Anything less, does not make art. The less belongs to "life and lifelessness" (pg. 230).

Extending the same note, Miller proclaims himself "inhuman," and belonging to the earth and to the race of the "inhuman ones, the race of artists" who move the "lifeless mass of humanity" by fever and ferment, to song...To be human is a poor, sorry, miserable affair, limited, restricted, defined...Sounding like Rimbaud, Miller calls for a world that produces ecstasy...And if we are all doomed—and he thinks it almost a certainty—

then let us, he continues, at least, howl and dance. "A last expiring dance" (pg. 232).

Dijon. Professor Miller. A job as teacher. No pay, but room and board. A "Franco-American amity arrangement" (pg. 234), Miller writes. "A job for a rich man's son" (pg. 234).

The town does not cut the mustard for Henry. A lugubrious atmosphere. The school does not cut it either.

Miller's resentments crop up into print. He becomes antagonistic. Against formal education; against the system of formal education; against the bastards who perpetuate the system of formal education; against the sons of bitches who participate in the system...He is in a foul mood, pissed-off; and has been since Paris, since he and Fillmore were run out of a catholic church during mass by a "bloated turnip-faced bastard" (pg. 240) of a priest. Nothing good to say about anything. A "bleak and empty" (pg. 250) town, bleak and empty school. A "scummy sterility" over the whole deal..."A bloody nightmare" he writes; one that he "could not throw off" (pg. 251).

NE France is in an unusually cold winter. "Everything frozen tight as scum" (pg. 253). The pipes of the school freeze, and the shit "piles up like ant hills" (pg. 254). The stench carries downwind for forty miles.

Henry's one consolation a kinship with the night watchman. The pions he has no use for. Whenever he sees one coming he hocks a juicy clam at their feet.

In springtime he escapes the "penitentiary" and returns to Paris, where Carl has lined up a job on the newspaper for him.

Carl and Van Norden are up to their usual tricks. Van Norden no longer goes with "cunts." He masturbates, making use of a cored-out apple and some cold cream. Carl is in Dutch for having relations with a fifteen year old girl. Fillmore is worse-off; he is in the nut house, diagnosed with "delusions of grandeur." He too has woman-trouble.

Seems he gave a French woman the clap then knocked her up. Fillmore says he wants to marry the woman (wants to do the "right thing") but the doctor advises against it. After he leaves the hospital, Fillmore gets engaged to Ginette. But is unhappy. Ginette brow-beats and his in-laws treat him like a slave. He wants out of the engagement but does not see how he can do it without Ginette, or his in-laws, murdering him. Henry steps in, telling Fillmore that he will take care of the situation. A wonderfully comic string of events follows after Fillmore puts himself into Henry's hands. First they go to the bank and withdraw all of Fillmore's money. Then to the British consulate for a visa. Then to the train station, and start of Fillmore's trip to London then the United States, where he can hear English spoken (which is his desire). Henry walks away with Fillmore's 2,800 francs. Money he is supposed to give Ginette. But will he? He sits by the river Seine, feeling the water flow through him. A wonderful peace falls over him, he says. Feels as if at the summit of a mountain. The Seine quietly flows: the course of the river, he says, "is fixed" (pg. 287).

In CANCER, Miller flays himself, like Michelangelo, stripping his outer layer to reveal the person beneath. An ugly person, perhaps, but also a "true" one. A picture of a man reduced by circumstance, become beggar and outcast, fed daily doses of humiliation and indifference...Without possessions, hope, or ambition...Can such a "man," if we can call him that—be content, even happy? "Henry Miller" is. Or says he is. A result, he claims, of his having died to the world and thereby been reborn, spiritually.

Not only happy, but the "happiest man alive." And who can deny that the ebullient, insouciant, and vital Henry Miller is not a portrait of a happy person? Like the famished miner, who strikes gold, Miller found the equivalent in finding himself. Previously, he only thought he was an artist: now he knows he is one, he relates.

Through an arduous process of reduction, nearing forty years old, he reaches nadir, and in doing so, is reborn. In death he finds life and is transformed. Becomes the exuberant "Henry Miller." The old brooding self-pitying Miller is, apparently, dead. The man who wanted more things instead of more life, is deceased. The man who sought himself through another (Mona) finds himself through being alone.

In this sense, CANCER is a profoundly optimistic book, because on the side of life. Miller is a man who says "yes" to life, and accepts rather than fights. Surrenders to life and thereby avoids the fate of the living death. Though sometimes seemingly little more than a huge intestine and genitals, he is alive in the spirit and flapping his wings, joyously—though in a universe of death.

AFTERWARD

If you get "into" Henry Miller, read all his works you can find, look into available biographical information, you quickly realize just how immense a figure of literature Miller was, and is: how deep a thinker, how great a writer, and how decent a human being. The breath of his erudition is staggering: a man who contained worlds, his interests straddling not only literature, but philosophy, spirituality, astrology, humanity, music, the visual arts, and more.

Unlike some celebrated American authors, Miller was not a he-man, in the sense of being "macho"; was not a hunter of big game, or a bar room brawler, or a two fisted drinker (preferred wine to other libations). Yet, he was a "man," all the same. "I am a man," he wrote in BLACK SPRING (pg. 22). "That seems to me sufficient."

He had no interest in traditional American sports of baseball, basketball, and football. He was a fan of prize-fighting and wrestling, making mention of the stars of his era in that arena (Jim Jeffries, Jack Johnson, Battling Siki, Tom Sharky, Jim Condos, Strangler Lewis, and others). Reportedly, when he lived in his Pacific Palisades house, where he lived after leaving Big Sur, he watched only one program on the TV: FRIDAY NIGHT WRESTLING (pg. 45, WHAT DONCHA KNOW? ABOUT HENRY MILLER, Twinka Thiebaud). Miller's main sporting interest was cycling. He was a follower of the world of cycling, and stories about time spent on his beloved bicycle are found throughout his work (wrote a tribute "MY BIKE," toward the end of his life).

Miller brought the language of the streets—admittedly, a male enclave—into literature, with publication of the TROPICS. Like Hamlin Garland, and Mark Twain (to a certain extent), Miller brought what was considered "common" usage of language into the rarefied air of "literature." He tramped into the drawing room, soiling the carpet with muddy feet. (This is not to imply that Miller was of the streets; personally, he was of a fastidious nature, and dressed in tailored suits—worn thin or sold in his improvident years in Paris – provided him by his father, a "boss" tailor.)

His work incidentally blazed a trail for freedom of expression. "Incidental" because he was not trying to blaze a trail, merely writing what he felt he had to write—getting rid of the poison in his guts, he claimed—sometimes in telepathic communication with his muse, which he referred to as "the Voice," or else, "it." Because of censorship of the prudes, particularly American puritans, his best work was banned for over twenty years in America. That he had to wait so long for a pay-off—nearly seventy years old when accumulated royalties from France were paid—was a shame.

Miller had a love/hate relationship to the Jewish people. Admiring Jews for their cultural accomplishments, and for having a feeling-toned existence foreign to Gentiles. He was in empathy with sorrowful Jewish history, but was also known to spout the usual shibboleths against Jews as avaricious money-grubbers (his mother referred to Jews as "Sheenies"). Miller had broad personal dealings with Jews, many Jewish friends, and worked closely with some (M. Fraenkel, W. Lowenfels)...His antipathy towards Jews stems from his childhood. After Jewish and Italian immigrants began crossing the newly built Williamsburg and Manhattan bridges and began to settle into the neighborhood where Henry lived as a child (Driggs Avenue, Fillmore Place, North First), the atmosphere of the neighborhood changed. Henry took personally the alteration, and blamed the Jews. His family's subsequent move, to Bushwick, in order to evade the immigrant influx, was a hard blow for Henry, who refused to attend school in his new district, instead returning to school in Williamsburg. Ferguson writes that Miller "gave a good impersonation of an anti-Semite in MOLOCH" (pg. 157, HENRY MILLER). An anti-Semitism, Ferguson adds, that pursued Miller into early manhood from childhood, where the primitive prejudice was learned, but was dropped by Miller after his world view and experience broadened.

Miller, at times, does sound like a "bloke," as critic Alfred Kazin once remarked. But what a bloke! What felicity! He could write like an angel, which, he claimed, he was (devil as well). As all of us are, he said; if only we knew it! If only we could enter into our divinity...But how? It's simple. All one has to do is die; die in the world, and begin to live in the spirit. "Life only commences at the hour of spiritual birth" (pg. 33, ALLER RETOUR NEW YORK, Henry Miller). From hopelessness—dead to the world and scraping bottom: "no money, no resources, and no hope" (CANCER, pg. 1), is the point at which one begins ascent to a higher realm of being, a spiritual realm, where one becomes angelic, divine, and only then, truly alive.

I consider Miller to be my spiritual grandfather. I can hear my maternal grandfather speaking whenever I read Miller. My grandfather used some of the same terms Miller used, terms regarded now as old-fashioned, many of them pejorative, such as Miller's use of the "N" word, and his term for black people, "darkies," commonly used by Anglos in early 20th century America—along with Mock, Mick, Wop, Hunky, Kraut, and other endearments, common coin of presumed Anglo-Saxon superiority. Also, Miller's use of the "N" word meant to designate any and every person of color; Miller was not a racist, not prejudicial in his personal life ("earth...not the home of the white or black or yellow or blue race...but the home of MAN, and all men equal" pg. 33, CAPRICORN). Nor was he particularly sexist, though he has taken a beating from feminists for his non-euphemistic language descriptive of the female. He was of an old-fashioned, or old world sensibility. I call him a "courtly misogynist." (This not written in an effort to excuse his behavior, but a plea, more or less, that he be judged as a product of his times.) "Woman…points the way." Miller wrote in SUNDAY AFTER THE WAR, pg. 160. "The masculine hegemony is over. Men have lost touch with the earth; they are clinging to the window-panes of their unreal superstructures like blind bats lashed by the storms of oceanic depths. Their world of abstraction spells babble."

Miller lived to ripe old age of 88. Mostly confined to bed his last year or so; blind in one eye and deaf in one ear, but, from accounts of that period (provided by Barbara Kraft and Twinka Thiebaud) still lively at the dinner table, still the raconteur, though repeating some of his stock-stories and occasionally nodding-out over the soup. His 5th marriage, this one to a Japanese "chanteuse" (pg. 16, Thiebaud) ended in divorce in 1977 (there was a separation seven years earlier), but Henry, the old romancer, had a girlfriend, a stunning and statuesque woman, a PLAYBOY centerfold, to whom he wrote 1500 letters, often professing his "love." Miller was in love with love. And the times in his life when he did not have someone to love, or a love-object, he became despondent (as in the interval between wife's #3 and #4). For a creative artist, like Miller, who spent much time alone, "a real relationship with a living, breathing, human being proved to be too much," wrote Thiebaud (pg. 29)...Considering the vacuity of his last years, raises an interesting question: did Miller, who liberated so many, liberate himself? Seems like an inordinate amount of self-torture late in his life. What can only be charitably called a marriage of convenience to a nightclub singer; a so-called relationship with a German translator, whom he sent, over the years, $40-60,000, receiving little or no consideration except the pleasure of giving; a one-sided love-affair with a "femme fatale" (pg. 27, Theibald) while he was mid-eighties...Did he ever break the fetters that bound him? Bound by his mother's dominance, his late-life search for love in whatever form—even solely in his own mind—suggests not. Suggests an incompleteness at the center of his character: that the wound of separation his mother's coldness created, never did heal.

It is time for me to leave Henry Miller, for now. Leave him as he shuffles out of the bedroom of his Pacific Palisades home, wearing a bathrobe and pajamas underneath, white socks, slippers: pushing a walker ahead of him (bad hips), one of his eyes half-closed in a squint, and a film of white hair circling his head. “Humm...” he intones, sniffing the aroma of food cooking on the stove, cooked by one of the sixteen cooks who alternate turns serving him...”Humm...Marvelous, doncha know,” he says in his Brooklynese. “Just marvelous.”

Wayne F. Burke, 2022

Selected Bibliography

Titles by Henry Miller:

TROPIC OF CANCER

TROPIC OF CAPRICORN

BLACK SPRING

SEXUS

PLEXUS

NEXUS

ALLER RETOUR NEW YORK

BOOKS IN MY LIFE

BIG SUR AND THE ORANGES OF HIERONYMUS BOSCH

SEXTET

TIME OF THE ASSASSINS

QUIET DAYS IN CLICHY

THE COLOSSUS OF MAROUSSI

THE WORLD OF LAWRENCE

MOLOCH

CRAZY COCK

THE AIR CONDITIONED NIGHTMARE

SUNDAY AFTER THE WAR

Additional Sources:

A SEASON IN HELL, Arthur Rimbaud

THE ILLUMINATIONS, Arthur Rimbaud

ARTHUR RIMBAUD: Presence of an Enigma, Jean-Luc Steinmetz (trans. By Jon Graham)

HENRY MILLER: The Last Days, Barbara Kraft, Sky Blue Press, San Antonio, TX, 2016

THE UNKNOWN HENRY MILLER, Arthur Hoyle, Arcade Publishing, NY, NY, 2014

HAPPIEST MAN ALIVE: A Biography of Henry Miller, Mary V. Deerborn, Touchstone Books, NY, NY, 1991

GENIUS & LUST, A Journey through the Major Writings of Henry Miller, Norman Mailer, Bantam Books, NY, 1977

THE DEVIL AT LARGE, Erica Jong, Grove Press, NY, 1993

WHAT DON'T CHA KNOW? ABOUT HENRY MILLER, Twinka Thiebaud, Elio Books, Beledere, CA., 2011

ALWAYS MERRY AND BRIGHT, The Life of Henry Miller, Jay Martin, Capra Press, Santa Barbara CA, 1978.

HENRY MILLER, A Life, Robert Ferguson, 1991, W. W. Norton & Co., NY, NY.

THE HISTORY OF ART, Elie Faure

Author's Note: Wayne F. Burke is, primarily, a poet who dabbles in prose. He is author of eight published full-length poetry collections—most recently BLACK SUMMER (SPARTAN Press, 2021). A book of his short stories, titled TURMOIL & Other Stories, was published in 2020 by Adelaide Press, NY, NY. For the past thirty-five years he has resided in the central Vermont area (USA).

www.ingramcontent.com/pod-product-compliance
Lightning Source LLC
Chambersburg PA
CBHW050021170726
48282CB00025B/495
9789390601974